# Welcome to
# Computers for
# ESL Students,
# 2nd Edition:
## Windows XP Version

**OLIVIA ADENDORFF**
Manteca Adult School

**LOIS WOODEN**
Manteca Adult School

## LABYRINTH
L E A R N I N G ®

President:
Brian Favro

Acquisitions Editor:
Jason Favro

Managing Editor:
Laura A. Lionello

Production Manager:
Rad Proctor

Editorial/Production Team:
Belinda Breyer, Arl Nadel, Wayne Popelka,
Televijay Technologies Pvt. Ltd., Sheryl
Trittin

Indexing:
Afterwords Editorial Services

Cover Design:
Huckdesign

**LABYRINTH**
L E A R N I N G ®

*Welcome to Computers for ESL Students, 2nd Edition: Windows XP Version*
by Olivia Adendorff and Lois Wooden

Labyrinth Learning
P.O. Box 20818
El Sobrante, California 94820
800.522.9746
On the web at www.lablearning.com

ITEM:        1-59136-196-6
ISBN-13:  978-1-59136-196-1


Manufactured in the United States of America.

0 9 8 7 6 5

# Table of Contents

# Preface

## What Is Covered

*Welcome to Computers for ESL Students, 2nd Edition: Windows XP Version* takes students with at least a low-intermediate ESL reading proficiency (as defined by the CASAS Skill Level Descriptors for ESL) through the basics of effectively using a computer to perform basic tasks. Using a highly visible approach combined with a wealth of individual and paired exercises, this book introduces students to beginning level skills and using computers that run Windows XP. This second edition includes coverage of Word 2007 and a new lesson on file management, as well as all new WebSims.

**Learning Objectives:** The global learning objective for this textbook is qualified by each student's reading level upon enrollment in the course.

| CASAS Reading Skill Level | Objective |
|---|---|
| High-intermediate or above | After completing a course with this textbook, students with a high-intermediate reading level should be able to study in a traditional beginner level computer course. |
| Intermediate or below | After completing a course with this textbook, students with less than a high-intermediate reading level should be able to continue learning using more advanced teacher-directed lessons. |

**About the Workbook:** An affordable workbook is available to complement this textbook. Student write directly in the workbook as they complete various individual and paired learning activities. It is highly recommended that each student have a copy of the workbook.

## What Is Different

For more than a decade, Labyrinth has been working to perfect our *unique instructional design.* The benefit of our approach is that learning is faster and easier for students. Instructors have found that our approach works well in self-paced, instructor-led, and "blended" learning environments. The Labyrinth approach has many key features, including the following.

• Concise concept discussions followed by exercises that give students experience with those concepts right away.

- Figures are always in close context with the text, so no figure numbers are necessary.

- Tables summarize key tasks with generic steps that will work without repeating exercises.

- Skill Builder exercises provide additional practice on key skills using less-detailed exercise steps as students progress through the lessons.

## Comprehensive Support

This course is also supported on the Labyrinth website with a comprehensive instructor support material package that includes detailed lesson plans, PowerPoint presentations, a course syllabus, extensive test banks, and more. Our unique WebSims allow students to perform realistic exercises with the web and email that would be difficult to set up in a computer lab.

We are grateful to the many instructors who have used Labyrinth titles and suggested improvements to us over the many years we have been writing and publishing books. Particularly, *Welcome to Computers for ESL Students, 2nd Edition: Windows XP Version* has benefited greatly from the reviews and suggestions of Barry Bakin, Pacoima Skills Center (Pacoima, CA); Ann Dwyer, South Seattle Community College (Seattle, WA); Alicia Nocum, Franklin Community Adult School (Los Angeles, CA); Lauren O'Brien, South Seattle Community College (Seattle, WA); Wesley Poplin, Wilkes Community College (Wilkesboro, NC); and Irma Sanders, Baldwin Park Adult & Community Education (Baldwin Park, CA).

# How This Book Is Organized

The information in this book is presented so that you master the fundamental skills first and then build on those skills as you work with the more comprehensive topics.

## Visual Conventions

This book uses many visual and typographical cues to guide you through the lessons. This page provides examples and describes the functions of each cue.

| | |
|---|---|
| `Type this text` | Anything you should type at the keyboard is printed in this typeface. |
| Menu→Command | This convention indicates how to give a command from the menu bar. For example, File→Save means to select File and then to select Save. |
| Command→<br>Command→<br>Command→etc. | This convention indicates how to give a command from the Ribbon. Commands are written Ribbon Tab→Command Group→Command→[subcommand]. |
|  | This icon indicates the availability of a web-based simulation for an exercise or other online content. You may need to use a WebSim if your computer is not set up to support particular exercises. |
|  | Vocabulary sections introduce nouns and verbs used in the lesson. |
|  | Exercises provide hands-on experience with each concept. |
|  | Skill Builders provide additional hands-on practice with moderate assistance. |
|  | Paired Conversations provide oral practice of practical conversations that include computer vocabulary terms and phrases. |

# Learning About Computer Basics

## LEARNING OBJECTIVES

After studying this lesson, you will be able to:

**Computer Objectives**

- Turn the computer on and off
- Identify the major parts of the computer
- Use the mouse

**Language Objectives**

- Use vocabulary words to describe parts of the computer
- Use computer verbs to describe actions
- Talk with a partner about the computer

*Additional learning resources are available at **labpub.com/learn/esl/complit2xp/***

# Vocabulary

## Picture Dictionary

The following nouns are introduced in this lesson:

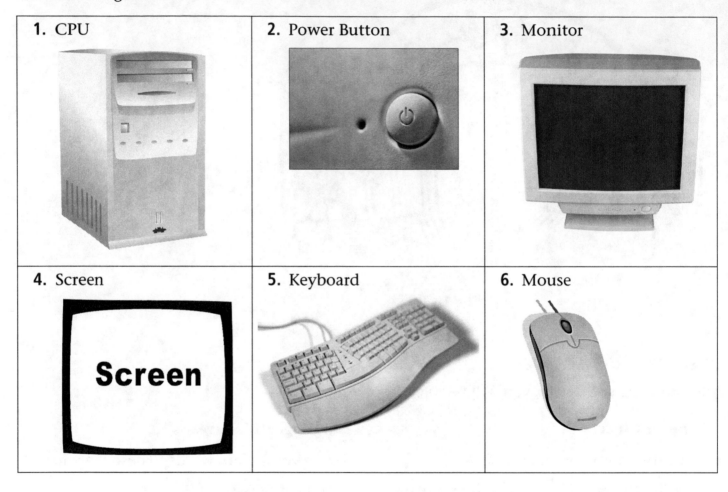

| 1. CPU | 2. Power Button | 3. Monitor |
| 4. Screen | 5. Keyboard | 6. Mouse |

1. **CPU (Central Processing Unit)** – The brain of the computer system

2. **Power Button** – The button that turns the computer on and off

3. **Monitor** – The part of the computer that you look at to see your work, like a television

4. **Screen** – The part of the monitor that lights up and shows what is happening on the computer

5. **Keyboard** – The part that you type on, which has all the letters, symbols, and functions

6. **Mouse** – The small oval piece that you can use to move from one part of the screen to another

# Picture Dictionary (continued)

| 7. Mouse Button | 8. Desktop | 9. Icon |
|---|---|---|
| 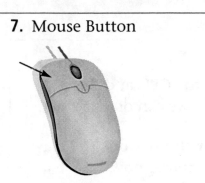 |  |  |

7. **Mouse Button** – The part at the top of the mouse (on the left) that you use to control the mouse

8. **Desktop** – The first thing you see on your screen when you turn on the computer

9. **Icon** – A picture that represents a program or command

# Computer Verbs

The following verbs are introduced in this lesson:

| TERM | MEANING | EXAMPLE |
|---|---|---|
| **1.** Turn on | To give power to the computer so that it works | Please turn on the CPU and the monitor so that we can do our work. |
| **2.** Turn off | To stop the power from going to the computer | I am finished with my work, so I can turn off the computer now. |
| **3.** Press | To push a button with your finger | If you want to turn on the computer, you have to press the power button. |
| **4.** Let go | To take your finger off the mouse button after you press it | When you use the mouse button, you have to press it and then let go. |
| **5.** Click | To press and let go of the mouse button (left side) in one smooth motion | Normally, you click the mouse button if you want to do something on the computer. |
| **6.** Go to | To take your mouse pointer to a place or program that you see on your screen | If you want to practice dragging, you can use the mouse to go to different icons and drag them on the screen. |
| **7.** Select | To choose a letter, word, sentence, paragraph, or program | I want to move that icon, so I will select it and drag it. |
| **8.** Shut down | To turn off the computer using the Start menu | I am finished with my work, so I will shut down the computer. |
| **9.** Drag | To use your mouse to take something to a different position | I don't like that icon in that corner. I need to drag it to a different place. |

# Concepts and Exercises

CONCEPT 1.1 **Computer Basics**

Computers are an important part of life today. It is important to learn to use them. They can be very useful at home and at work.

Here are some common things that you can learn to do:

- Type a personal or business letter

- Make a picture

- Find maps and driving directions

- Find information that you need for school or work reports

- Send and receive information from other people, even in other countries

- Add, subtract, multiply, and divide numbers

## CONCEPT 1.2  Parts of the Computer

Here are the parts of a computer system. Each one has its own special job.

**A. CPU** – The CPU (Central Processing Unit) is where all the "thinking" is done. Some people call it a tower. CPUs come in different shapes and sizes.

Figure coourtesy of 123RF™

**B. Monitor** – The CPU uses the monitor to give you information. It shows you what the computer is doing.

**C. Speakers** – The speakers let you hear the sounds that the computer makes.

**D. Keyboard** – You use the keyboard to put numbers and letters into the computer.

**E. Mouse** – The mouse lets you point at and select different things on the computer screen.

 EXERCISE 1.2  **Find Computer Parts**

In this exercise, you will find the parts of the computer.

**1.** Sit down at a computer.

**2.** Look at the picture of the parts of the computer in this book. Find those parts on your computer.

## CONCEPT 1.3 The Correct Way to Sit at the Computer

It is important to sit correctly when using the computer so you do not hurt after using it.

**A.** Sit up straight in your chair.

**B.** Keep your wrists straight.

**C.** The top of the monitor should be at the same level as your eyes.

**D.** Sit with your feet flat on the floor.

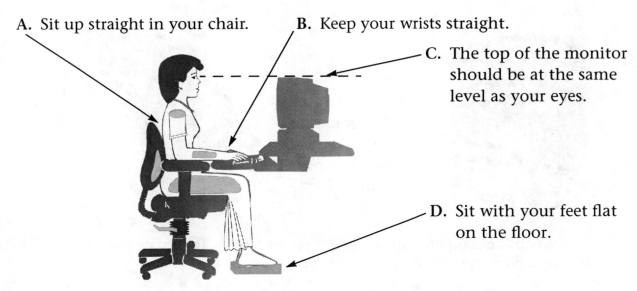

The Correct Way to Sit at a Computer

 ## EXERCISE 1.3 Sit at the Computer Correctly

In this exercise, you will sit at the computer in the correct way.

1. Sit in a chair in front of a computer. Put your hands on the keyboard.

2. Ask your partner to check your sitting position. You should have your feet, back, wrists, and eyes in the correct positions.

CONCEPT 1.4 **Turning On the Computer**

On the front of the CPU, you will see some slots and some buttons. Each one has a special job.

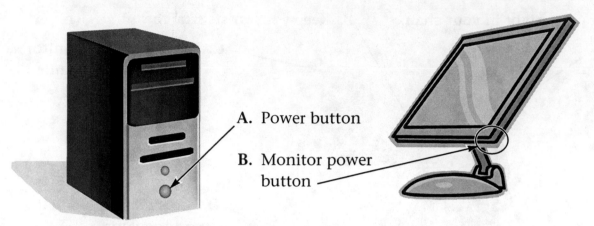

**A.** Power button

**B.** Monitor power button

To turn on the computer, press the CPU power button. To turn on the monitor, press the monitor power button.

 EXERCISE 1.4 **Turn On the Computer**

In this exercise, you will practice turning on the computer and the monitor.

1. Find the power button on the CPU of a computer in your classroom.

2. Push it, and listen for the computer to come on. You should hear a beep as it warms up.

3. Push the power button on the monitor to turn it on.

Once the computer and monitor have been on for a few minutes, you should see the Windows Desktop.

## CONCEPT 1.5 What Is Windows?

Windows is a special program that you can use to communicate with the CPU. Windows must be put onto the computer before you can do anything on the computer. The CPU uses Windows to communicate in a language that you can understand. It also tells the other programs and machines that are attached to the computer, such as the printer, what to do.

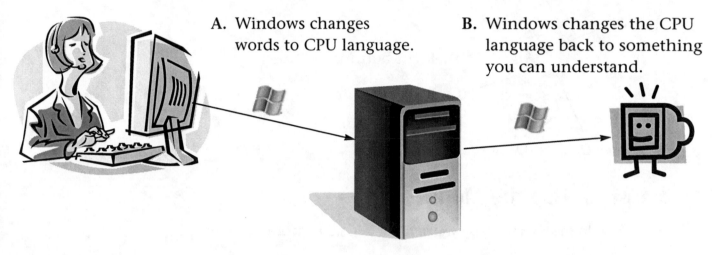

**A.** Windows changes words to CPU language.

**B.** Windows changes the CPU language back to something you can understand.

 EXERCISE 1.5 **Move the Mouse Pointer**

In this exercise, you will move the mouse on the Windows Desktop.

**1.** Look at the screen. It should look similar to the next screen. (It may have a different picture on it or none at all.)

Windows
Desktop

**2.** Move your mouse around and watch the mouse pointer (the small arrow) move on the screen.

 Mouse
Pointer

**Using a Mouse**

The mouse is used to point at things on the screen. It is called a mouse because the cord looks like a tail.

- You usually use the left button of the mouse.

- If you need to use the right button, you will be told to right-click.

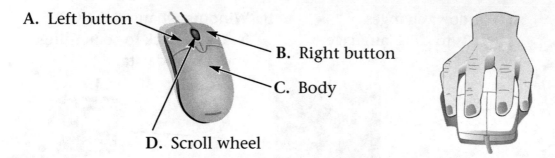

A. Left button

B. Right button

C. Body

D. Scroll wheel

 EXERCISE 1.6 **Use the Mouse**

In this exercise, you will practice using the mouse.

1. Hold the sides of the mouse with your thumb and fourth finger. You should have one finger on each button. Do not hold it too tightly!

2. Put the bottom part of your hand on the mouse pad.

3. Move the mouse around, and watch the mouse pointer move on the screen.

4. Move the mouse so the pointer is on top of one of the icons on the desktop. Click (press, then let go of) the left mouse button one time, and see the color change on the icon.

   This is how the icon should look after you click on it.

   Recycle Bin

5. Put your mouse on top of one of the icons. Hold down the left button and move the mouse. You should see the icon move to a new place when you let go. This is called dragging.

   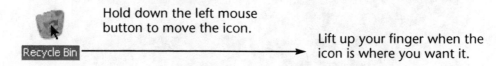
   Hold down the left mouse button to move the icon.

   Recycle Bin

   Lift up your finger when the icon is where you want it.

6. Practice dragging icons to different parts of the Desktop.

CONCEPT 1.7 **Turning Off the Computer**

To keep the computer working correctly, you must turn it off correctly.

Start→Turn Off Computer→Turn Off

This is an example of a command. When you give a command, you tell the computer to do something for you.

 EXERCISE 1.7 **Turn Off the Computer**

In this exercise, you will practice turning off the computer.

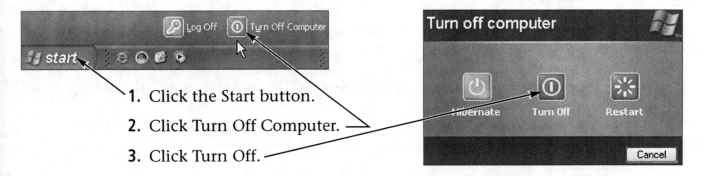

1. Click the Start button.
2. Click Turn Off Computer.
3. Click Turn Off.

4. Do not push the power button on the CPU. It will go off by itself.

# Skill Builder Exercises

SKILL BUILDER 1.1 **Turn On the Computer**

1. Press the power button on the CPU. Listen for the computer to beep.

2. Press the power button on the monitor.

---

SKILL BUILDER 1.2 **Drag Icons**

1. Use your mouse to drag all the icons on the Desktop to the bottom-right corner.

2. Use your mouse to drag all the icons on the Desktop to the top-right corner.

3. Use your mouse to drag all the icons on the Desktop to the left side.

---

SKILL BUILDER 1.3 **Turn Off the Computer**

1. Click the Start button.

2. Click Turn Off Computer.

3. Click Turn Off.

4. Press the power button on the monitor to turn it off. Do not push the power button on the CPU. It will go off by itself.

---

**Personal Project: Describe Computer Parts**

1. On a piece of paper, make a list of all the parts of a computer system.

2. Describe in your own words what each one looks like. Write one sentence about each one.

---

 **Conversation**

## Paired Conversation

With a partner, take turns reading the A and B parts of the conversation.

| | |
|---|---|
| Student A | Hi. What's that? |
| Student B | This is my new computer. |
| Student A | Really? How exciting! |
| Student B | Let me show you. This is the CPU. |
| Student A | I know. It's the brain. |
| Student B | That's right! This is the monitor. |
| Student A | Wow! It has a nice screen. |
| Student B | I know. This is called the keyboard. |
| Student A | Yeah, I know that word. My brother takes keyboarding at school. |
| Student B | This is the mouse and these are the mouse buttons. |
| Student A | What a cute mouse. Can I push the button? |
| Student B | Not yet! You have to turn on the computer first. |
| Student A | OK. Can I push the power button to turn it on now? |
| Student B | Sure. The first thing you see is the Desktop. |
| Student A | The colors look good. |
| Student B | I know. I love my new computer! |
| Student A | You are so lucky! |

# Using Windows and the Start Menu

## LEARNING OBJECTIVES

After studying this lesson, you will be able to:

### Computer Objectives

- Identify the parts of a program window
- Use the Start menu to open a program
- Move a window using the mouse
- Minimize, maximize, restore, and close a window

### Language Objectives

- Talk with a partner about the different parts of a window
- Talk about how to find and use different buttons, bars, and menus
- Describe how to move a window and use the sizing buttons

*Additional learning resources are available at labpub.com/learn/esl/complit2xp/*

 **Vocabulary**

# Picture Dictionary

The following nouns are introduced in this lesson:

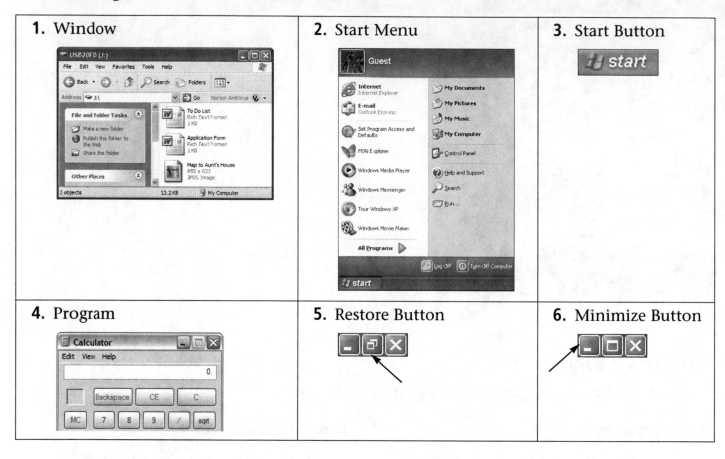

| 1. Window | 2. Start Menu | 3. Start Button |
| --- | --- | --- |
| 4. Program | 5. Restore Button | 6. Minimize Button |

1. **Window** – A rectangular area on the screen that shows a program or message

2. **Start Menu** – The list that appears when you click on the Start button; it shows the main programs

3. **Start Button** – The button on the bottom-left corner of your screen that opens the Start menu

4. **Program** – A set of directions (such as Microsoft Word, computer games, Calculator, and WordPad) that tells the computer what to do to get a job done

5. **Restore Button** – The button in the same place as Maximize that changes a large window to a smaller size

6. **Minimize Button** – The button that looks like a minus sign at the top-right of a window. It makes the window disappear, but the program is still open

# Picture Dictionary (continued)

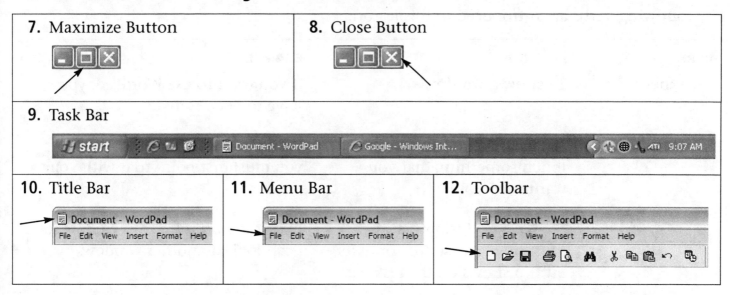

**7.** Maximize Button

**8.** Close Button

**9.** Task Bar

**10.** Title Bar

**11.** Menu Bar

**12.** Toolbar

7. **Maximize Button** – The square button between Minimize and Close that makes a window fill the whole screen

8. **Close Button** – The button with an "x" that closes the window; it makes the window disappear and also closes the program

9. **Task Bar** – The bar at the bottom of the screen that shows all open programs

10. **Title Bar** – The bar at the very top of a window that shows the name of the program you are using

11. **Menu Bar** – The bar with words that is below the title bar and gives you ways to use the program

12. **Toolbar** – A bar showing different icons; each icon does a different job when you click on it

# Computer Verbs

The following verbs are introduced in this lesson:

| VERB | MEANING | EXAMPLE |
|------|---------|---------|
| 1. Open | To show a window | If you want to use WordPad, you have to open it first. |
| 2. Point | To make the mouse pointer touch something that you want to choose | When you want to select an icon, you must first point to it with your pointer. |
| 3. Minimize | To make a window disappear (but not close) so that only its button shows on the task bar | I want to minimize this window so I can look at another window. |
| 4. Restore | To change a maximized window to a smaller size | I'm going to restore this window because I don't want it to be so big. |
| 5. Maximize | To make the window larger so that it fills the entire screen | I need to maximize my window because I want it to be as big as possible. |
| 6. Close | To stop a program. It will not show on your screen anymore | Class is finished. Please close your windows and turn off your computers. |

# Concepts and Exercises

CONCEPT 2.1 **The Windows Desktop**

The Windows Desktop appears when you turn on the computer. Sometimes it shows a picture. It has these main parts:

A. **Icons** – Pictures that represent programs or commands

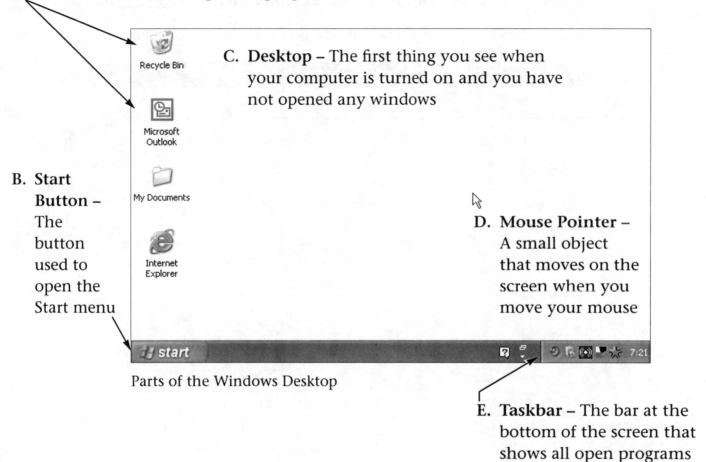

C. **Desktop** – The first thing you see when your computer is turned on and you have not opened any windows

B. **Start Button –** The button used to open the Start menu

D. **Mouse Pointer –** A small object that moves on the screen when you move your mouse

Parts of the Windows Desktop

E. **Taskbar** – The bar at the bottom of the screen that shows all open programs

EXERCISE 2.1  **Use the Windows Desktop**

In this exercise, you will learn to use the Windows Desktop.

1. If necessary, turn on the computer.
   You should see the Windows Desktop on the screen.

2. Move your mouse, and watch the mouse pointer move on the screen.

3. Point (don't click) with your mouse pointer over the Recycle Bin 🗑 .

4. Point (don't click) with your mouse pointer over the 🏁 start button.

5. Point (don't click) with your mouse pointer over the task bar.

CONCEPT 2.2 **Opening a Program**

You use the Start button to start programs with the Start menu.
The Start menu shows the programs the computer can run. The
Start menu also allows you to do other things, such as turn off the computer.

EXERCISE 2.2 **Start the WordPad Program**

In this exercise, you will use the Start button to start the WordPad program.

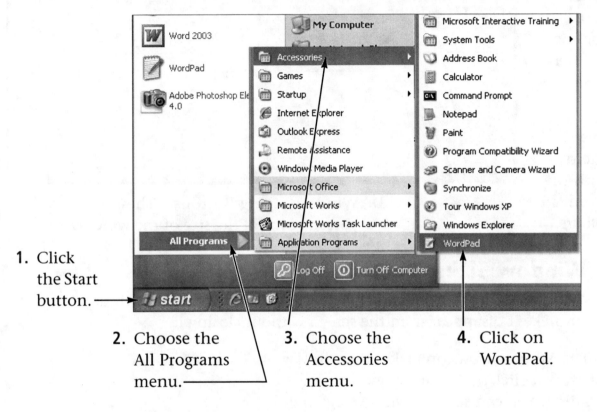

1. Click
   the Start
   button.

2. Choose the
   All Programs
   menu.

3. Choose the
   Accessories
   menu.

4. Click on
   WordPad.

5. Leave the WordPad window open.

**Parts of a Program Window**

Most program windows have parts similar to what you see on the screen in WordPad. Look at the picture below to identify the different parts.

**A. Title Bar** – The title bar is always at the very top of the window. It tells you the name of the program you are using.

**B. Menu Bar** – The menu bar gives you choices of things to do; it is different in different programs.

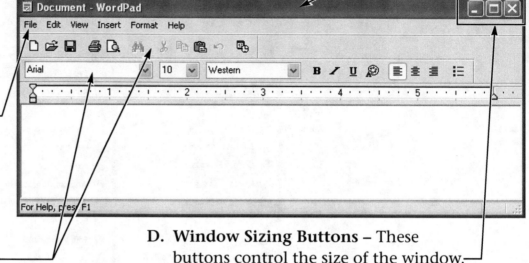

**C. Toolbars** – Toolbars have buttons to help you work with the program. WordPad has two toolbars.

**D. Window Sizing Buttons** – These buttons control the size of the window.

# Window Sizing Buttons

Window sizing buttons can change the size of the program window, close it, or make it disappear from the screen without closing it.

**A. Minimize** – The Minimize button makes the window disappear when you click on it. The window is not closed, just hiding. You can see that window again if you click its button on the task bar.

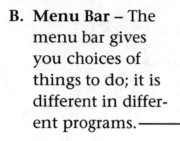

**B. Maximize** – When you click on the Maximize button, it makes the window fill the whole screen.

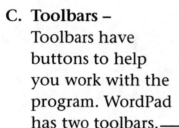

**D. Close** – The Close button closes the window and the program.

**C. Restore** – When you click the Restore button, the window returns to the size it had before it was maximized.

EXERCISE 2.3  **Work with WordPad**

In this exercise, you will look at features of the WordPad program window and use the window sizing buttons.

**NOTE!**  Do not click in steps 1–6; just point at parts of the WordPad window.

1. Using your mouse, put your mouse pointer on (don't click) the toolbar.

2. Put your mouse pointer on the menu bar (don't click).

3. Put your mouse pointer on the title bar.

4. Put your mouse pointer on the Minimize button.

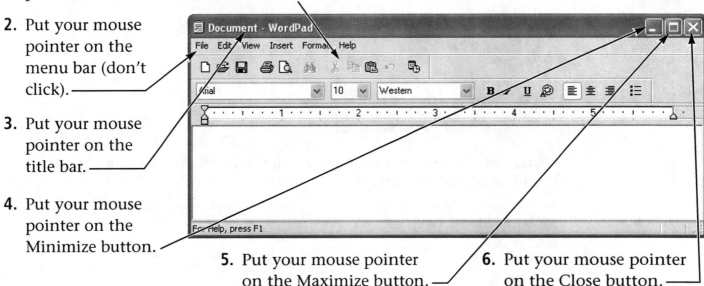

5. Put your mouse pointer on the Maximize button.

6. Put your mouse pointer on the Close button.

7. Minimize WordPad by clicking the Minimize button.

   Look at the bottom of the screen. You will see a WordPad button on the task bar. You did not close WordPad, you just hid the window.

8. Click the WordPad button on the task bar to make that window show again.

9. Click the Maximize button to make WordPad fill the whole screen.

10. Click the Restore button to make WordPad smaller.

11. Click the Close button to close WordPad.

## CONCEPT 2.4 Moving a Window

Sometimes you will want to move a window to see all of it better or to see something underneath it.

---

**HOW TO MOVE A WINDOW**

- If the window is already maximized, click the Restore 🗗 button. You cannot move a window if it is maximized to fill the whole screen.

- To move a window, you must put your mouse pointer on the title bar of the window.

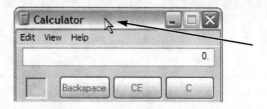

- Hold down the left mouse button and move the mouse. You can move the window in any direction.

---

EXERCISE 2.4 **Open the Calculator Program**

In this exercise, you will open the Calculator program and move the Calculator program window.

1. Open the Calculator program: Start→All Programs→Accessories→Calculator.

## Move the Calculator Window

2. Put your mouse pointer on the title bar.

4. Release the mouse button.

3. Hold down the left mouse button and move the calculator window up.

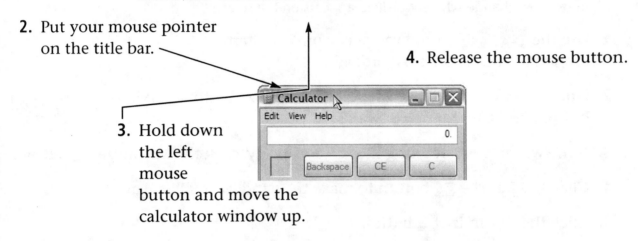

5. Hold down the mouse button while it is on the title bar, and keep it held down as you drag to the left. Then let go of the mouse button.

7. Hold down the mouse button and drag down. Let go of the mouse button.

6. Hold down the mouse button and drag to the right. Then let go of the mouse button.

8. Close the Calculator using the Close ☒ button.

# Skill Builder Exercises

**SKILL BUILDER 2.1** **Open and Close WordPad**

In this exercise, you will practice opening the WordPad program. Then you will use buttons to change where WordPad appears on the screen.

**1.** Use the 🛑 start button to open WordPad: Start→All Programs→Accessories→WordPad.

**2.** Find the title bar, toolbar, menu bar, Minimize button, Maximize button, and Close button.

**3.** If the window is not filling the screen already, click the Maximize 🔲 button.

**4.** Click the Restore 🗗 button to make the window smaller again.

**5.** Click the Minimize 🗕 button.

**6.** Click the 🗐 Document - WordPad button on the task bar to restore the window.

**7.** Click the Close ❎ button to close WordPad.

---

**SKILL BUILDER 2.2** **Move a Window**

In this exercise, you will open the Calculator program and move it on the screen.

**1.** Open the Calculator program: Start→All Programs→Accessories→Calculator.

**2.** Put your mouse pointer on the title bar.

**3.** Hold down the mouse button and move the calculator to the top-right of the Desktop. Release the mouse button.

**4.** Move the calculator to the bottom-right of the Desktop.

**5.** Move the calculator to the top-left of the Desktop.

**6.** Move the calculator to the bottom-left of the Desktop.

**7.** Move the calculator to the center of the Desktop.

**8.** Close ❎ the Calculator program.

---

SKILL BUILDER 2.3  **Open and Move the Notepad Window**

In this exercise, you will open the Notepad program and move it on the screen.

1. Open Notepad: Start→All Programs→Accessories→Notepad.

2. Find the title bar and the menu bar.
Notice that Notepad does not have a toolbar.

3. Find the Minimize ⬛, Maximize ⬛, and Close ✖ buttons.

4. Click the Maximize ⬛ button to make the Notepad window fill the screen.
Notice that the Maximize button turns into the Restore button.

5. Click the Restore ⬛ button to make the window smaller again.

6. Click the Minimize ⬛ button.

7. Click the ⬛ Untitled - Notepad button on the task bar to restore the window.

8. Put your mouse pointer on the title bar, and move the Notepad window to different places on the Desktop.

9. Close ✖ the Notepad program.

---

SKILL BUILDER 2.4  **Personal Project: Draw Computer Parts**

In this exercise, you will draw the parts of the computer.

1. On a piece of paper, make a list of six computer words that you know.

2. Draw a picture next to each one to show what it means.

3. Show your words and pictures to other students in your class. Look at their work too.

---

 **Conversation**

## Paired Conversation

With a partner, take turns reading the A and B parts of the conversation.

| | |
|---|---|
| Student A | Good morning. |
| Student B | Hi. What are we studying today? |
| Student A | I think we are going to learn how to open and close a window. |
| Student B | Do you mean if the temperature gets too hot in here? |
| Student A | No! I mean to open a window on our computers. |
| Student B | My computer doesn't have any windows. It only has a screen. |
| Student A | Don't be silly! There are windows inside your computer. |
| Student B | Oh! How do you open a window? |
| Student A | Well, we will learn that today. |
| Student B | Will we have to use the Start button? |
| Student A | Yes, and the Start menu too. |
| Student B | That will be interesting. |
| Student A | We'll learn about different parts of a window. |
| Student B | I know about the title bar. |
| Student A | That's great. You'll learn about the menu bar, too. |
| Student B | What else is important to learn? |
| Student A | Well, the toolbar tells you what tools you can use. |
| Student B | I can't wait to start! |

# Using Windows Programs

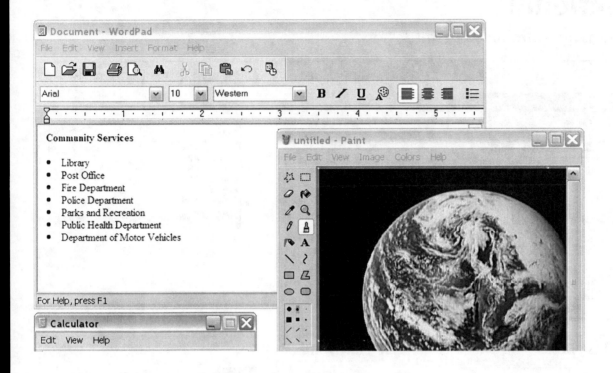

## LEARNING OBJECTIVES

After studying this lesson, you will be able to:

### Computer Objectives

- Open a dialog box and work with a drop-down list

- Draw a picture in the Paint program

- View and zoom to a larger size

- Use the Calculator program

### Language Objectives

- Use vocabulary words to describe parts of different programs

- Use computer verbs to describe actions you can do with different programs

- Talk with a partner about drawing a picture in the Paint program

- Talk with a partner about the different things you can do with programs

*Additional learning resources are available at **labpub.com/learn/esl/complit2xp/***

# Vocabulary

## Picture Dictionary

The following nouns are introduced in this lesson:

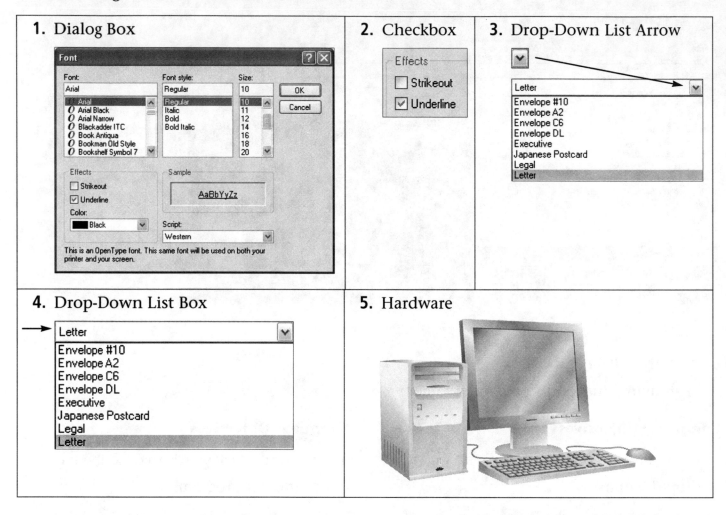

**1. Dialog Box**

**2. Checkbox**

**3. Drop-Down List Arrow**

**4. Drop-Down List Box**

**5. Hardware**

1. **Dialog Box** – A window with boxes you can check to select what you want

2. **Checkbox** – A box that you can check to select something that you want

3. **Drop-Down List Arrow** – An arrow that you can click to make the drop-down list box appear

4. **Drop-Down List Box** – A list with more things you can choose from

5. **Hardware** – The physical part of the computer system, such as the monitor or the keyboard

# Picture Dictionary (continued)

**6.** Software

**7.** Appearance

**8.** Settings

---

**6. Software** – Everything in the computer system that is not hardware, such as WordPad

**7. Appearance** – The way something looks

**8. Settings** – Information about how a program is set up

# Computer Verbs

The following verbs are introduced in this lesson:

| VERB | MEANING | EXAMPLE |
|------|---------|---------|
| 1. Appear | When something shows and you can see it | When you click the box, a checkmark will appear inside the box. |
| 2. Check | To click a box so that a checkmark appears | When you have a few choices, you have to check the one that you want. |
| 3. Clear (a box) | To click a button or box to remove what you checked before; to uncheck a box | I changed my mind, so I have to clear the box that I checked before. |
| 4. Release (a button) | To take your finger off the mouse button | After you finish your mouse action, you should release the mouse button. |
| 5. Let up | To release or let go of the button | Another way to say "release the mouse button" is to say "let up on the mouse button." |
| 6. Play | To use a computer game | I like to play Solitaire and other card games on my computer. |
| 7. Preview | To see how information will look when it is printed so you can decide what you want to do | If you look at the Preview on the screen, you can see how the document will look when you print it. |
| 8. Hold (a button) | To keep your finger pressed on the mouse button | Sometimes you have to hold down your mouse button for a few seconds, and sometimes you only have to tap it. |
| 9. View | To look at something | It is important to view the tools on the toolbar so you can see what you can use. |

# Concepts and Exercises

**Common Features in Programs**

A *program* is a set of directions that tell the computer exactly what to do to get a special kind of job done. Not all programs look the same.

Here are examples of kinds of programs that do different jobs:

A *word processing program* is used to type text.

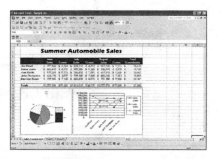

A *spreadsheet program* is used mostly for numbers.

A *graphics program* is used to make and change pictures.

A *web browser* is used to find things on the Internet.

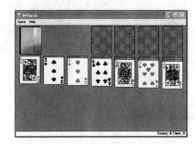

A *computer game* is used to relax and have fun.

A *tutorial* is used to show and teach ideas.

Different programs have many parts that are the same. Most program windows have the following parts:

A. **Title Bar** – Tells you what program you are using

B. **Menu Bar** – Lists commands that let you do different things to your work

C. **Toolbar** – Has icons that do different things when you click them

D. **Work Area** – The place where your work shows when you put it in by typing or using the mouse

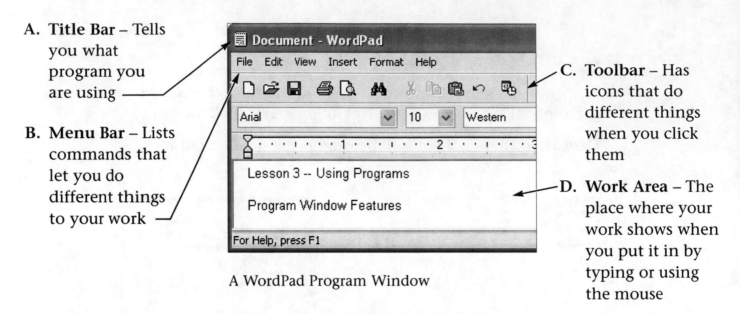

A WordPad Program Window

A. **Title Bar** – Tells you what program you are using

B. **Menu Bar** – Lists commands that let you do different things to your work

C. **Tool Box** – Similar to a toolbar and used in many drawing programs such as Paint

D. **Work Area** – The place where your work shows when you put it in by typing or using the mouse

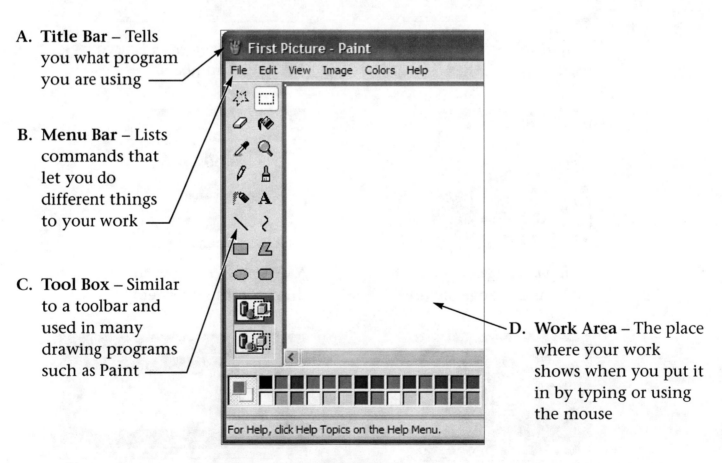

A Paint Program Window

EXERCISE 3.1  **Open the Paint Program**

In this exercise, you will use the Start button to start the Paint program. Every computer with Windows has this program.

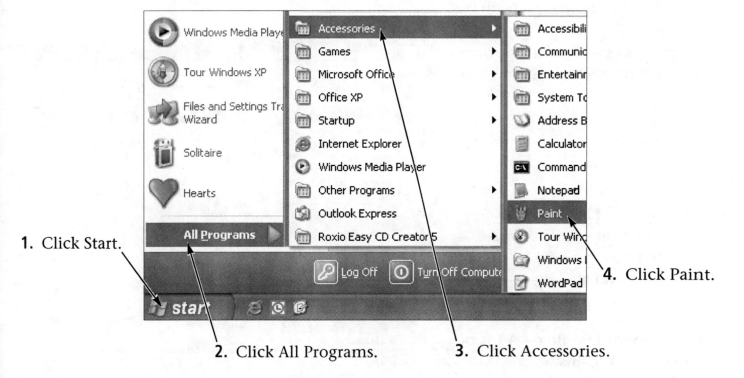

1. Click Start.

2. Click All Programs.

3. Click Accessories.

4. Click Paint.

5. Click the Maximize ⊡ button to make the Paint window fill the screen.

6. Find the title bar on the screen, and point at it with the mouse.
   See page 22 if you have trouble finding this or other parts of the window.

7. Find the menu bar, and point at it with the mouse.

8. Find the Tool Box. (The toolbar in Paint is called a Tool Box; it has a different shape from most toolbars.) Show your partner.

**Dialog Boxes**

Most programs have some type of dialog box. You can change settings by changing the information in a dialog box. Many dialog boxes have the following features:

**A. Checkboxes** – Click in the boxes to check or uncheck them.

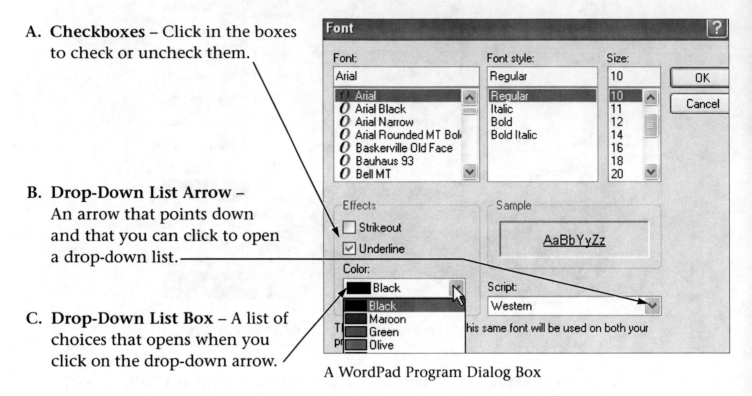

**B. Drop-Down List Arrow** – An arrow that points down and that you can click to open a drop-down list.

**C. Drop-Down List Box** – A list of choices that opens when you click on the drop-down arrow.

A WordPad Program Dialog Box

EXERCISE 3.2  **Open a Dialog Box**

In this exercise, you will use a dialog box in Paint.

1. Choose File on the menu bar. ———→

2. Choose Page Setup.———————→

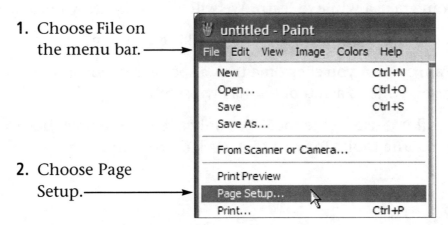

The following dialog box will appear on your screen.

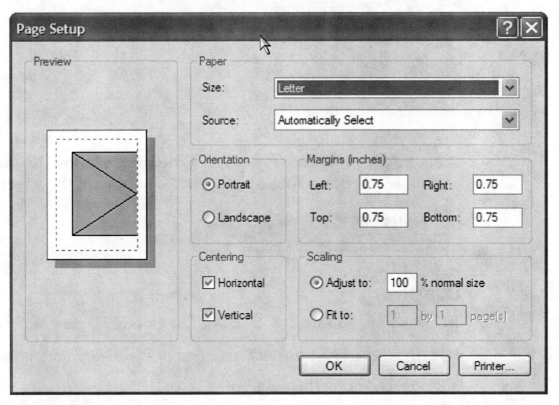

Paint Dialog Box

3. Find a drop-down arrow, drop-down list box, and a checkbox.

4. Close the dialog box with the Close ⊠ button. Do not close Paint.

**Using Tools on a Toolbar**

Paint gives you many tools to work with to make pictures. Some are easy to use. Some take a while to learn. We will look at the easy ones now.

- You can use tools on a toolbar by clicking on them.

- In Paint, when you click on a tool, a special symbol appears in place of the mouse pointer. Each tool has its own symbol.

- We will not use all the tools, but only a few to see how they work. Here are some of the tools. To use a tool, click on the tool.

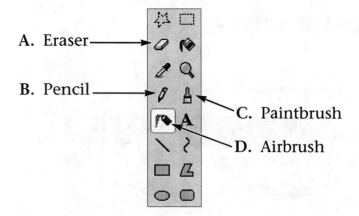

A. Eraser

B. Pencil

C. Paintbrush

D. Airbrush

Tools only work in the white area of the Paint window. If you want to pick a color, click on one of the colors near the bottom of the screen.

## Dragging

To use a tool, you need to drag with the mouse. Here is how:

- Point where you want to start; then hold down your left mouse button.

- Move the mouse to make your design.

- Let go of the left mouse button when you are finished making the design.

You will learn how to drag in the next exercise.

**Use Tools in Paint**

In this exercise, you will practice using some of the drawing tools. Paint should still be open from the last exercise.

### Draw a Line

**2.** Point to a place on the left side of the white area. Hold down your left mouse button, and keep it held down until step 4.

**3.** Move the mouse to the right. This draws a line.

**1.** Click the Line tool in the Tool Box.

**4.** Let go of the mouse button where you want to stop the line.

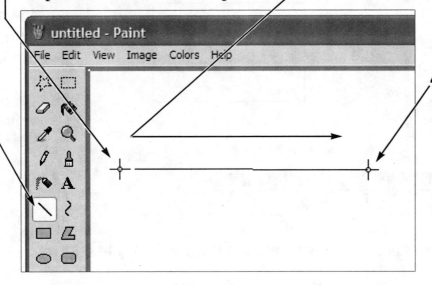

You should see a line.

### Draw a Box

**5.** Click the Rectangle tool.

**6.** Point to a place anywhere on the white area. Hold down the mouse button and move it in the direction shown while keeping the button held down.

**7.** Let go of the mouse button.

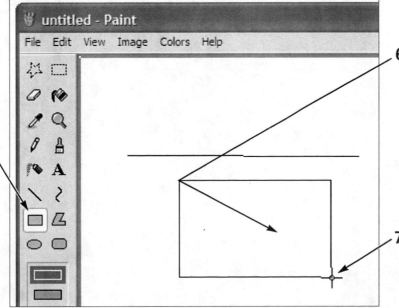

**Draw a Colored Line**

**8.** Click the Airbrush tool.

**9.** Click the color red from the Color Box.

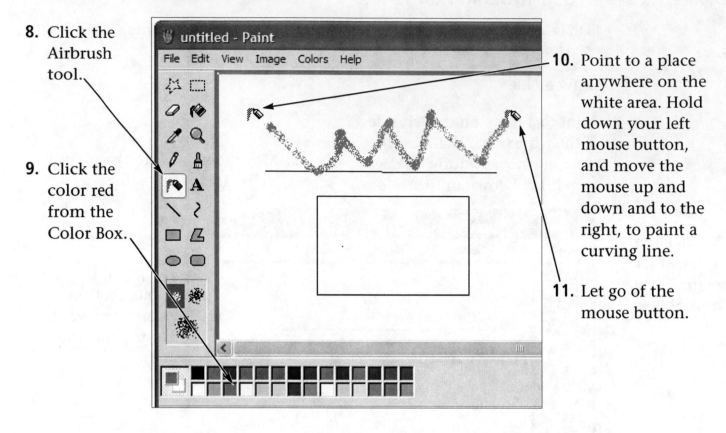

**10.** Point to a place anywhere on the white area. Hold down your left mouse button, and move the mouse up and down and to the right, to paint a curving line.

**11.** Let go of the mouse button.

**12.** You can keep drawing to add anything else you like to your picture.

**13.** When you are finished, leave Paint open.

CONCEPT 3.4  **Using a Menu**

Once you have some practice using menus, they are easy to use. The way they work is the same from one program to the next. What changes in each program is the list of choices in the menu.

- You can open a menu by clicking on one of the words.

- Each word has its own menu that opens separately.

- When you click on some of the menu items, a dialog box will open.

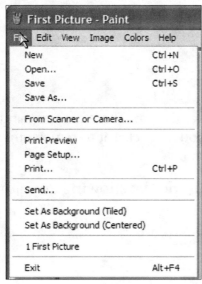

Paint's File menu. It opens when you click File.

Paint's View menu. It opens when you click View.

EXERCISE 3.4 **Use a Menu**

In this exercise, you will learn how to use a menu. Many settings can only be changed by using menus.

1. Click View on the menu bar. Keep your mouse over the View menu item.

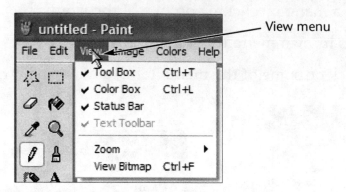

See that many of the items have a check by them. These are the things that are already showing. To make a toolbar not show, you must click it to remove the check. In the next step, you will turn off the Tool Box setting.

2. Click Tool Box. The Tool Box should not be showing anymore.

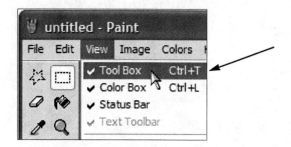

Now the Tool Box disappears, as shown in the next picture.

To make the Tool Box show again, you must click it on the menu so it is checked.

3. Click View, and then choose Tool Box. Make sure the Tool Box is showing again.

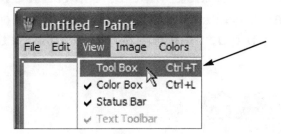

4. To see your picture larger, click View→Zoom→Large Size.

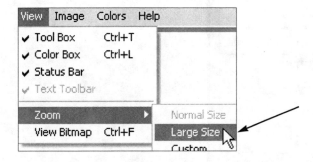

5. To see it at its normal size again, click View→Zoom→Normal Size.

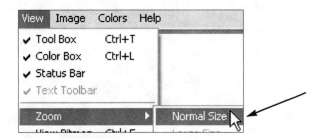

6. Close ☒ Paint.

7. When Paint asks if you want to save your work, click No.

## CONCEPT 3.5 The Windows Calculator

The Calculator is a useful tool on the computer. You can use it to do many calculations. The program looks just like a regular handheld calculator and works the same way. You can type numbers, or you can click the number buttons.

## HOW TO USE THE CALCULATOR

### Open the Calculator

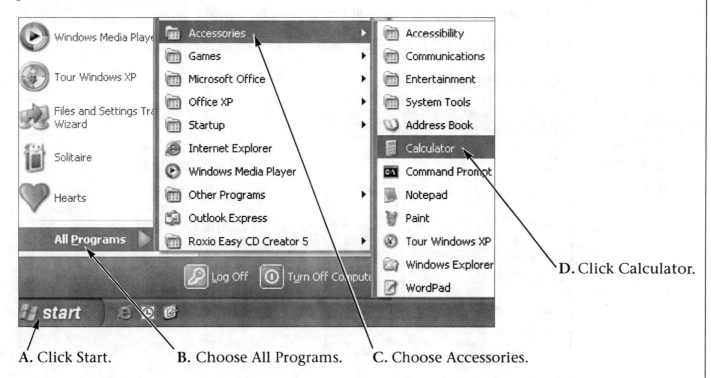

A. Click Start.　　B. Choose All Programs.　　C. Choose Accessories.

D. Click Calculator.

| Add Two Numbers | Subtract Two Numbers |
|---|---|
| A. Click the first number. | A. Click the first number. |
| B. Click the plus + sign. | B. Click the minus − sign. |
| C. Click the second number. | C. Click the second number. |
| D. Then click the equal = sign. | D. Then click the equal = sign. |

**Multiply Two Numbers**

- To multiply, use the * button (3 * 2 = 6).

**Divide Two Numbers**

- To divide, use the / button (8 / 2 = 4).

To clear a number from the Calculator, click the C (Clear) key.

EXERCISE 3.5 **Use the Calculator**

In this exercise, you will use the Calculator to add and subtract. You do not have to type in the numbers. Just click the number buttons with your mouse.

1. Open Calculator: Start→All Programs→Accessories→Calculator.

### Add Two Numbers

2. Click the 2 button two times for 22.

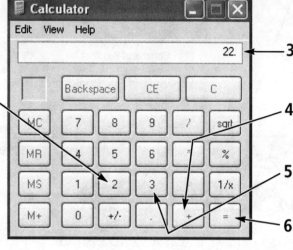

3. See the number in the number box.

4. Click the plus sign to add the next number.

5. Click the 3 button two times for 33.

6. Click the equal sign (=) to finish.

You can see the answer (55) in the number box.

7. Click the C button to clear the Calculator.

### Do Other Calculations

Press C to clear after you complete each of the calculations in steps 8–11.

8. 12 + 6 =

9. 100 + 75 =

10. 50 – 10 =

11. 389 – 14 =

12. Close the Calculator.

# Skill Builder Exercises

SKILL BUILDER 3.1 **Use Paint**

In earlier exercises, you tried some Paint tools. In this exercise, you will create a real drawing.

1. Open Paint with Start→All Programs→Accessories→Paint.

2. Maximize 🔲 the Paint window.

3. Use the menu bar to make the Tool Box go away by clicking View→Tool Box.

4. Use the menu bar to make the Tool Box show again by clicking View→ Tool Box.

5. Use some of the tools and colors to draw a picture of a house.

   The house doesn't have to look perfect. This is just to practice using the mouse and dragging to draw. Many programs let you do this.

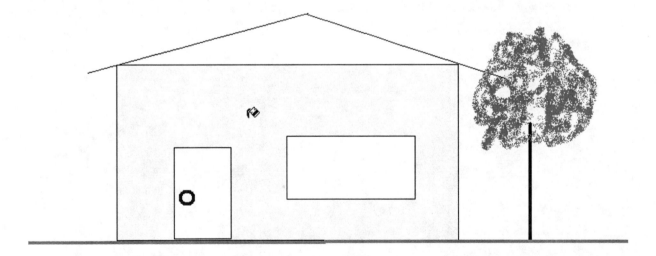

6. When you are finished, Close 🗙 Paint.

7. When it asks you if you want to save your work, click No; or if you already know how to save a file, click Yes and give the file a name.

   ⚠️**NOTE!** You will learn how to save your files in Lesson 5, Doing More with WordPad.

## SKILL BUILDER 3.2 Use Calculator

In this exercise, you will use the Calculator program to multiply, divide, and subtract numbers.

1. Open Calculator: Start→All Programs→Accessories→Calculator.
2. Multiply: $3 \times 12 =$
3. Multiply: $25 \times 2 =$
4. Divide: 80 ÷ (use /) 4 =
5. Divide: $36 \div 12 =$
6. Subtract: $99 - 43 =$
7. Subtract: $52 - 12 =$
8. Close the Calculator using the Close button.

**Play a Game**

In this exercise, you will learn to play Solitaire. If you have never played Solitaire with cards, ask a friend or your teacher to explain how to play the game. Playing this game will give you good practice using the mouse.

1. Open Solitaire with Start→All Programs→Games→Solitaire.

2. To move one of the cards, click on it. Hold down the mouse button and drag it to a new place. If you put a card in the wrong place, it will not stay there. It will jump back to where it was.

3. When you want to turn over a new card, click on the pack at the top.

4. Start putting the aces in the four shaded areas, and build up from there. The suits (pictures on the cards) must match in each top pile. You must put all the cards in the top piles in order to win.

5. If you want to start a new game, click Game→Deal.

6. When you are finished playing, click the Close ☒ button.

**Personal Project: Draw a Map**

In this exercise, you will draw and print a simple map with the Paint program.

**1.** Start the Paint program: Start→All Programs→Accessories→Paint.

**2.** Draw lines to create a simple street map of the area around your house.

!**TIP!** To draw straight lines, hold down the ⌈Shift⌋ key as you drag a new line.

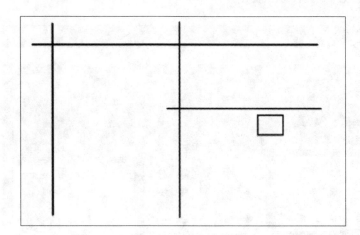

**3.** Use the Text **A** tool to add street names. Click near where you want to type the words. Hold down the mouse button and drag a text box. Then you can type a street name inside the box. Make a new box for each name.

| | |
|---|---|
| | Main Street |
| First Street | |
| | Ponderosa Street |

**4.** Click File→Print, and then click Print to print the map.

**5.** If you know how to save a file, use File→Save As to save it. Or you can close the Paint program without saving the map.

# Conversation

## Paired Conversation

With a partner, take turns reading the A and B parts of the conversation.

| | |
|---|---|
| Student A | Yesterday we learned how to minimize a window. |
| Student B | Yes, I remember. The window disappeared but did not really close. |
| Student A | Do you remember how to maximize a window? |
| Student B | Yes. Now, let's talk about what we learned today, too. |
| Student A | Today we learned about hardware. |
| Student B | Is that like the computer and the monitor? |
| Student A | Right. We also learned about software. |
| Student B | That's like WordPad and Paint. |
| Student A | That's true. |
| Student B | We also learned about the dialog boxes. |
| Student A | Yes. Dialog boxes are important. |
| Student B | What about settings? |
| Student A | Settings are easy to change. They decide so many things. |
| Student B | Did you play a computer game today? |
| Student A | Not really. I just watched somebody else play. |
| Student B | We did practice how to check boxes. |
| Student A | Then we learned how to uncheck to clear the boxes. |
| Student B | Well, I'm so glad that we remember so much! |

# Creating a Document in WordPad

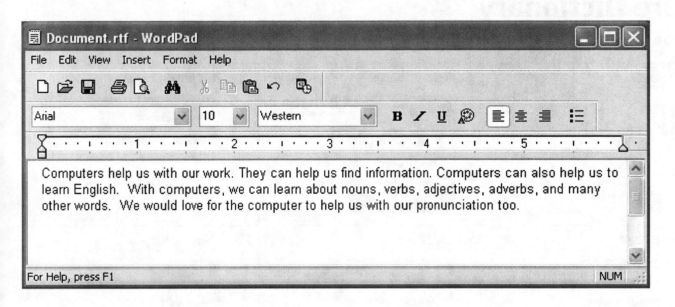

```
Document.rtf - WordPad                                    [_][□][X]

File   Edit   View   Insert   Format   Help

 D  ☞ 🖫  🖨 🔍  🏛   ✂ 📋 📋 ↶ 🔁

Arial            ▼  10  ▼  Western            ▼  B  𝐼  U  🖉  ≡  ≡  ≡  ☰

    · · · 1 · · · · · · 2 · · · · · · 3 · · · · · · 4 · · · · · · 5 · · · · ·

Computers help us with our work. They can help us find information. Computers can also help us to
learn English.  With computers, we can learn about nouns, verbs, adjectives, adverbs, and many
other words.  We would love for the computer to help us with our pronunciation too.

For Help, press F1                                                    NUM
```

## LEARNING OBJECTIVES

After studying this lesson, you will be able to:

**Computer Objectives**

- Use the computer keyboard
- Use WordPad

**Language Objectives**

- Use vocabulary words to discuss using WordPad and the keyboard
- Use computer verbs to describe how to use WordPad and the keyboard
- Use computer language to talk about how to create a document

*Additional learning resources are available at **labpub.com/learn/esl/complit2xp/***

 # Vocabulary

## Picture Dictionary

The following nouns are introduced in this lesson:

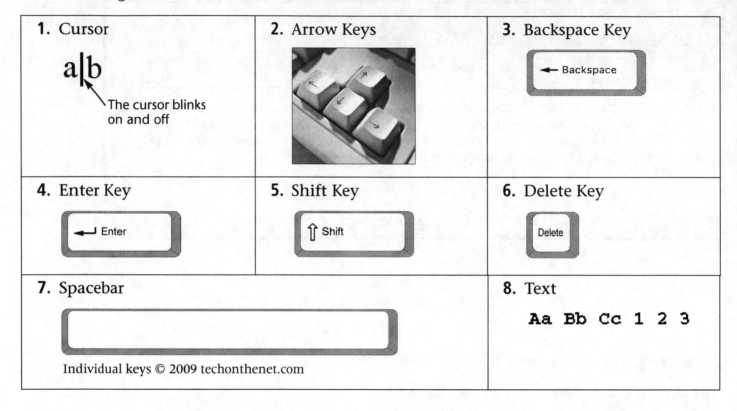

| 1. Cursor | 2. Arrow Keys | 3. Backspace Key |
|---|---|---|
| a\|b  The cursor blinks on and off | | ← Backspace |
| 4. Enter Key | 5. Shift Key | 6. Delete Key |
| ←⎵ Enter | ⇧ Shift | Delete |
| 7. Spacebar | | 8. Text |
| Individual keys © 2009 techonthenet.com | | Aa Bb Cc 1 2 3 |

1. **Cursor** – An object on the screen that shows where you are going to type text

2. **Arrow Keys** – Keys that move your cursor to another place without erasing

3. **Backspace Key** – A key that erases what is behind the cursor

4. **Enter Key** – A key that moves the cursor to the next line

5. **Shift Key** – A key that makes a capital letter or the top symbol of the typed key

6. **Delete Key** – A key that erases what is in front of it

7. **Spacebar** – The bar that puts a space between words

8. **Text** – The words and letters that you type on the keyboard

# Picture Dictionary (continued)

**9.** Printer

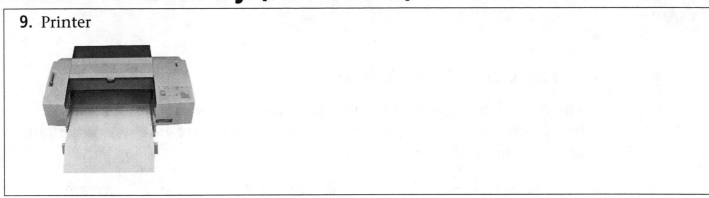

**9.** A machine that puts informaton from the computer onto a sheet of paper

# Computer Verbs

The following verbs are introduced in this lesson:

| VERB | MEANING | EXAMPLE |
|---|---|---|
| **1.** Enter | To go to the next line or paragraph when typing text | To enter is to move to the next line when typing text. |
| **2.** Delete | To take away or erase | I typed the wrong word. I will delete it and type the correct word. |
| **3.** Type | To use the keyboard to put information on the page | I don't know how to type, so I have to take a keyboarding class. |
| **4.** Wrap | To make words automatically continue onto the next line | When you type a paragraph, the computer will wrap the words onto the next line. |
| **5.** Insert (text) | To type text between two other letters or words | I forgot to type my middle name. I need to insert it between my first name and last name. |
| **6.** Print | To put a document from your computer onto a sheet of paper | I finished my letter. Now I will print it and mail it to my grandmother. |

# Concepts and Exercises

CONCEPT 4.1 **The Computer Keyboard**

The computer keyboard has more keys than a typewriter has. In this lesson, you will be using only the common keys. Here are some important keyboard keys.

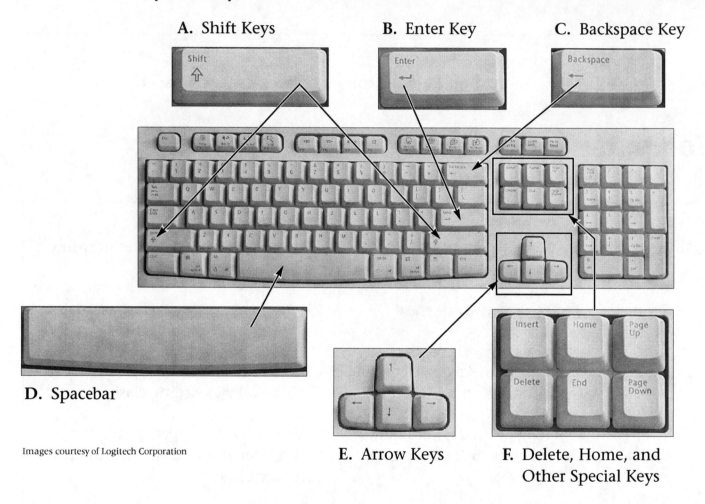

**A.** Shift Keys    **B.** Enter Key    **C.** Backspace Key

**D.** Spacebar

Images courtesy of Logitech Corporation

**E.** Arrow Keys    **F.** Delete, Home, and Other Special Keys

**Examine the Computer Keyboard**

In this exercise, you will find the keys on the computer keyboard.

⚠️ **NOTE!** Your keyboard may not look exactly like the one on this page.

**1.** Look at the computer keyboard.

**2.** Look at the top row of keys. None of them are on a typewriter.

**3.** Find the Backspace key.

**4.** Find the Delete key.

**5.** Find a Shift key.

**6.** Find the Spacebar.

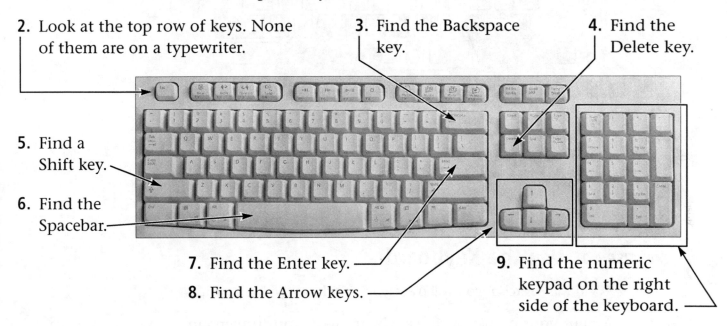

**7.** Find the Enter key.

**8.** Find the Arrow keys.

**9.** Find the numeric keypad on the right side of the keyboard.

## CONCEPT 4.2  Using the Keyboard

Typing on a keyboard is important to learn to do well. The best way is to take a keyboarding class. Your hands should rest on the keyboard like this.

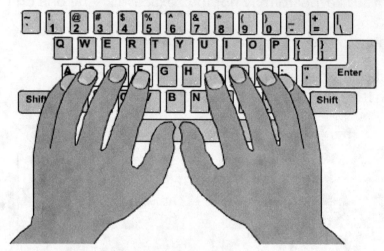

Image courtesy of learn-everything.com

## EXERCISE 4.2  Use the Keyboard

In this exercise, you will place your hands on the keyboard.

1. Put your hands on the keyboard with your fingers on the keys as shown above. You should feel a small bump on both the F and J keys.

2. Move your fingers up or down to touch the other keys.

**Word Processing Programs**

A word processing program helps you write on the computer. You can write letters, notes, lists, and many other things. There are two commonly used word processing programs.

| | WordPad | A simple word processing program that comes with every Windows computer |
| | Word | A powerful word processing program that you must buy separately and install on a computer |

 EXERCISE 4.3 **Start the WordPad Program**

In this exercise, you will use the Start button menu to start the WordPad program. Then you will look at the WordPad program window.

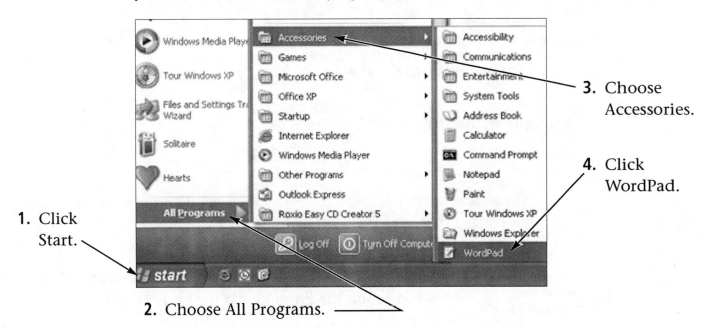

1. Click Start.

2. Choose All Programs.

3. Choose Accessories.

4. Click WordPad.

WordPad opens on the screen.

5. Find the title bar, menu, and toolbars on the WordPad window.

6. Leave the WordPad program open and continue with the lesson.

**Typing on the Computer**

You type on the computer with the keyboard. Everything you type appears at the cursor position.

### The Cursor

The cursor is a blinking line that shows where the computer will type next. You can move the cursor anywhere you have typed. You will learn how to move it soon.

### Word Wrap

When you are typing and reach the end of a line, the computer will automatically put the next words you type on the next line for you. That is called word wrap.

- Example with Word Wrap

```
Computers help us with our work. They
can help us find information. Computers
can also help us to learn English.
```

- Example without Word Wrap

```
Computers help us with our work. They can help us find
```

### Enter Key

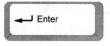

The Enter key starts a new line wherever the cursor is. You only need to use the Enter key at the end of a short line or a paragraph.

### Spacebar

The spacebar is used to make a space between words.

EXERCISE 4.4  **Type with WordPad**

In this exercise, you will turn on the word wrap setting in WordPad. Then you will type.

**1.** Click View→Options to open the Options dialog box.

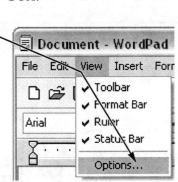

**2.** Click the Rich Text tab.

**3.** Click in the circle next to Wrap to Ruler.

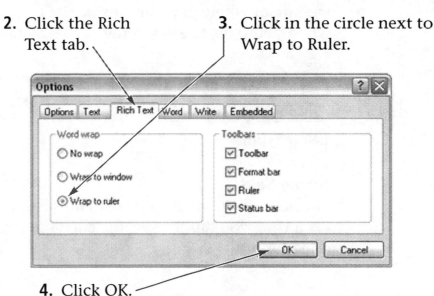

**4.** Click OK.

**5.** Type the sentences in the following paragraph. Do not press ⌈Enter⌉. When there is not enough space on the line, the words will go to the next line. Hold the ⌈Shift⌉ key down to make capital letters.

```
Computers help us with our work. They can help us find
information. Computers can also help us to learn English.
With computers, we can learn about nouns, verbs, adjectives,
adverbs, and many other words. We would love for the
computer to help us with our pronunciation too.
```

This is how your screen should look when you are finished.

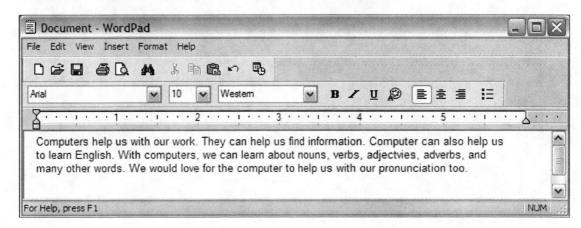

## CONCEPT 4.5 **Inserting Text**

You can insert text by moving the cursor and then typing. You must first put the cursor where you want, using the mouse or the arrow (cursor) keys. Then when you type, the new letters appear where the cursor is blinking.

Cursor —

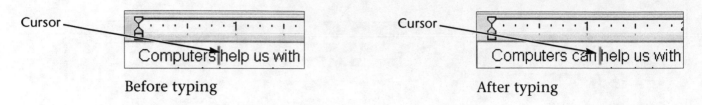

Computers|help us with

Before typing

Cursor —

Computers can|help us with

After typing

### Arrow Keys

The arrow keys on the keyboard are also called cursor keys. Each time you tap the key, the cursor moves once in that direction.

**Insert Text**

In this exercise, you will insert a word and insert new lines into your WordPad document.

**1.** Click to the left of the word "help."

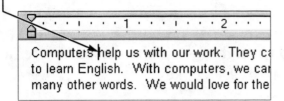

**2.** Type **can** and Spacebar.

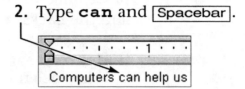

Now you will make two blank lines.

**3.** Move your mouse to the left of the "C" in "Computers." Click only when you see the mouse pointer change to a ].

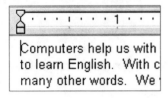

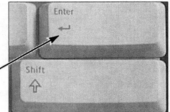

**4.** Press the Enter key, then press Enter again to make two new lines.

**5.** Press the up arrow key two times (to get to the top of the document).

Now you are ready to type a new line in step 6.

**6.** Type the new line **Typing in a Word Processor** here. ————

Typing in a Word Processor

Computers can help us with our us to learn English. With compu many other words. We would lov

It is easy to add new lines or words at any time.

**Deleting Text**

You can delete (remove) letters, words, and even entire lines from a word processing document. There are two main ways to do this: use the Delete key and the Backspace key.

### Delete Key

This key deletes letters to the right (→) of the cursor. You remove one letter or space each time you tap the Delete key.

A. Cursor

B. [Delete] [Delete]
   [Delete] [Delete]

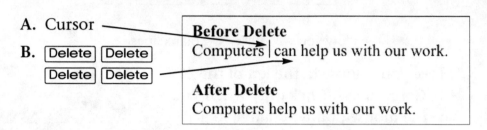

**Before Delete**
Computers | can help us with our work.

**After Delete**
Computers help us with our work.

### Backspace Key

This key deletes letters to the left (←) of the cursor. You remove one letter or space each time you tap the Backspace key.

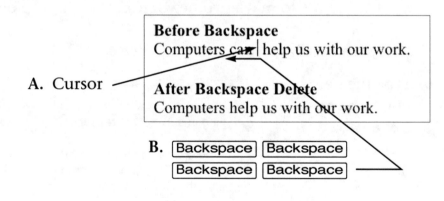

**Before Backspace**
Computers can| help us with our work.

A. Cursor

**After Backspace Delete**
Computers help us with our work.

B. [Backspace] [Backspace]
   [Backspace] [Backspace]

EXERCISE 4.6 **Delete Text**

In this exercise, you will delete some words from your document. Then you will close the WordPad program.

### Use the Delete Key

**1.** Click to the left of the word "can" in the second line of text.

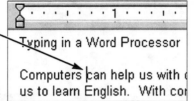

**2.** Press [Delete] [Delete] [Delete] [Delete] so the word "can" and the space after it are erased.

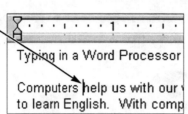

### Use the Backspace Key

**3.** Click to the right of the sentence "They can help us find information."

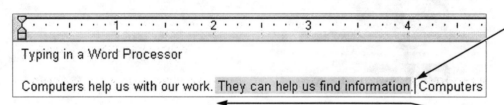

**4.** Press the [Backspace] key until the whole sentence is gone and one more time to take out the extra space.

This is what the screen should look like after step 4.

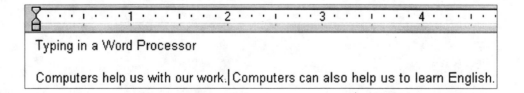

## CONCEPT 4.7 Printing Your Work

You will often want to print documents that you type. Most programs have two methods you can use to give the print command. Both methods send what is open on your screen to the printer.

- Click File→Print on the menu bar.

- Or, click the Print  button on the toolbar.

- Your computer sends the document to the printer and the printer puts it onto the paper.

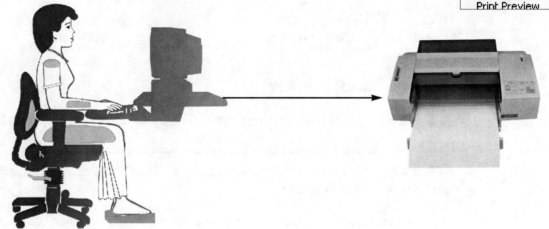

EXERCISE 4.7  **Print Your Document**

In this exercise, you will add your name to your WordPad file, save it, and then print it.

1. Use the arrow keys or the mouse to go to the very bottom of your WordPad document text.

2. Press the ⌈Enter⌉ key two times.

3. Type your name at the bottom of the document.

4. Click File→Print from the menu bar.

5. When the Print window opens, click Print or OK to finish the command.

6. Go to the printer and get your document.

7. Close ⌧ the WordPad window.
   WordPad will ask if you wish to save changes to your document.

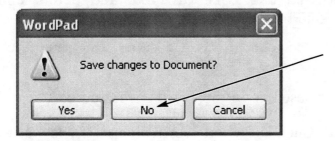

8. Click No to close the WordPad program without saving your document.
   You will learn how to save your documents in Lesson 5, Doing More with WordPad.

# Skill Builder Exercises

SKILL BUILDER 4.1 **Type Sentences**

In this exercise, you will type a simple document with WordPad.

1. Open WordPad: Start→All Programs→Accessories→WordPad.

2. Type the following sentences.

   Use the `Shift` key to make capital letters. Only press the `Enter` key where it appears below.

   **The cursor shows where you are going to type text.** `Enter`
   `Enter`

   **You use a keyboard when you want to put letters or numbers into the computer.** `Enter` `Enter`

   **The Shift key lets you type a capital letter or the top symbol on a key.** `Enter` `Enter`

   **Press the Enter key when you want to start typing text on another line.** `Enter` `Enter`

   **Arrow keys are used to move to another place without erasing.** `Enter` `Enter`

   **Place the cursor to the left of text and press the Delete key to erase.** `Enter` `Enter`

   **Place the cursor to the right of text and press the Backspace key to erase.** `Enter`

3. Print your work. Choose File→Print from the menu bar.

4. Close ⊠ WordPad. Click No when WordPad asks if you want to save your work.

---

**Make a List**

In this exercise, you will type a list of punctuation marks with WordPad. Then you will insert a title for the list.

1. Open WordPad: Start→All Programs→Accessories→WordPad.

2. Type the following sentences.

   You must use the ⌈Shift⌉ key to type some of the punctuation marks. Only press the ⌈Enter⌉ key where it appears below.

   **. A period is used at the end of a statement or a command.**
   ⌈Enter⌉

   **, A comma is used to separate words or phrases.** ⌈Enter⌉

   **: A colon is used to introduce a list.** ⌈Enter⌉

   **! An exclamation mark is used at the end of a sentence that shows surprise or strong feeling.** ⌈Enter⌉

   **? A question mark is used at the end of every sentence that asks a question.** ⌈Enter⌉

   When you finish, your screen should look like this:

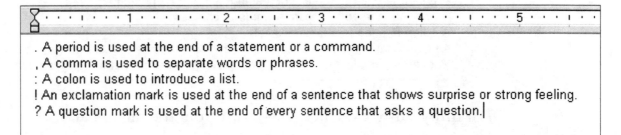

### Insert a Title for the List

**3.** Put the cursor at the top-left of the list. (Use the arrow keys.)

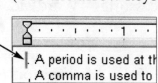

**4.** Press the Enter key two times.

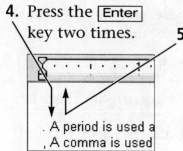

**5.** Press the Up Arrow key two times (to move the cursor to the top).

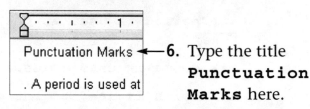

**6.** Type the title **Punctuation Marks** here.

Now your screen should look like this:

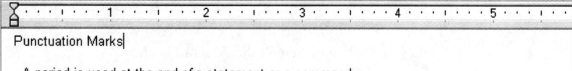

Punctuation Marks

. A period is used at the end of a statement or a command.
, A comma is used to separate words or phrases.
: A colon is used to introduce a list.
! An exclamation mark is used at the end of a sentence that shows surprise or strong feeling.
? A question mark is used at the end of every sentence that asks a question.

**7.** Print your work. Click File→Print from the menu bar.

**8.** Close ☒ WordPad.

**9.** Click No when WordPad asks if you wish to save your work.

You will learn how to save your work in Lesson 5, Doing More with WordPad.

SKILL BUILDER 4.3 **Type a Paragraph**

In this exercise, you will type a paragraph with WordPad.

1. Open WordPad: Start→All Programs→Accessories→WordPad.

2. Type the following paragraph.
   Do not press [Enter] until the end of the paragraph. Let Word Wrap move your words to the next line for you. Your lines will probably end at different places than they do in this example.

   **Notepad is a program that comes with Windows. It is very simple and can be used to put words and numbers into the computer. It cannot check spelling or grammar. It does not have toolbars like WordPad.** [Enter]

3. Print your work. Choose File→Print from the menu bar.

4. Close ⊠ WordPad.

5. Click No when WordPad asks if you wish to save your work.

---

SKILL BUILDER 4.4 **Personal Project: Type a To-Do List**

In this exercise, you will type a list of things to do. Then you can print the list.

1. Open WordPad: Start→All Programs→Accessories→WordPad.

2. Read the following instructions, and then start to type a list:
   - In complete sentences, type a list of things that you want to do tomorrow.
   - Be sure to start with a title.
   - Type a list of five things that you want to do (one on each line).
   - Use the [Enter] key at the end of each line.

3. Print your work. Choose File→Print from the menu bar.

4. Close ⊠ WordPad.

5. Click No when WordPad asks if you wish to save your work.

---

 # Conversation

## Paired Conversation

With a partner, take turns reading the A and B parts of the conversation.

| | |
|---|---|
| Student A | Hello. Are you learning to use the computer? |
| Student B | Yes, I am. |
| Student A | Will you show me how to type a letter to my sister? |
| Student B | Yes. First, open the WordPad program. |
| Student A | I don't know how to do that. |
| Student B | Click the Start button. Go to All Programs, Accessories, then click WordPad. |
| Student A | Oh! I see "WordPad" on the title bar! |
| Student B | Do you see the cursor blinking on the screen? |
| Student A | Yes, I do. |
| Student B | The computer is telling you that it is ready for you to type your text. |
| Student A | Is there anything else that I should know before I start? |
| Student B | Yes. At the end of a paragraph, press the Enter key. |
| Student A | OK. Anything else? |
| Student B | When you want a capital letter, hold the Shift key down and type the letter. |
| Student A | Oh. That's good to know. |
| Student B | You can also erase a word with the Backspace key. |
| Student A | Thanks so much for helping me. |
| Student B | I'm sure your sister will be happy to get your letter. |

# Doing More with WordPad

## LEARNING OBJECTIVES

After studying this lesson, you will be able to:

**Computer Objectives**

- Save a file
- Name a file
- Format and align text in various ways
- Add bullets to a list

**Language Objectives**

- Use appropriate words to describe saving and naming files
- Describe how to format and align text
- Tell a partner how to perform tasks learned in this lesson

*Additional learning resources are available at **labpub.com/learn/esl/complit2xp/***

## Picture Dictionary

The following nouns are introduced in this lesson:

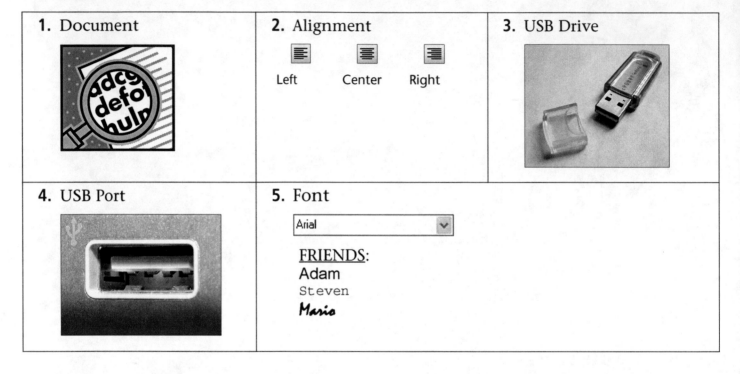

| 1. Document | 2. Alignment | 3. USB Drive |
| --- | --- | --- |
| | Left    Center    Right | |
| 4. USB Port | 5. Font | |
| | Arial | |
| | FRIENDS:<br>Adam<br>Steven<br>Mario | |

1. **Document** – Something that is written and provides information

2. **Alignment** – How text is placed, on either side or in the center

3. **USB Drive** – A small tool used to save computer files; you can use it in different computers

4. **USB Port** – A small opening on the CPU where you insert a USB drive

5. **Font** – The design and size of the letters

# Picture Dictionary (continued)

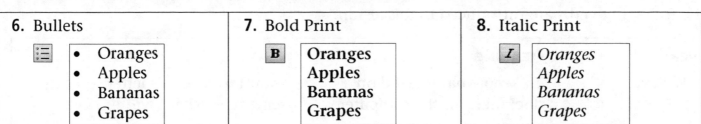

| 6. Bullets | 7. Bold Print | 8. Italic Print |
|---|---|---|
| • Oranges<br>• Apples<br>• Bananas<br>• Grapes | **Oranges**<br>**Apples**<br>**Bananas**<br>**Grapes** | *Oranges*<br>*Apples*<br>*Bananas*<br>*Grapes* |

**6. Bullets** – Special dots, squares, checkmarks, or characters that you can put before items on a list

**7. Bold Print** – A style of lettering where the letters are thicker and darker

**8. Italic Print** – A style of lettering where the letters are a little slanted to the right

# Computer Verbs

The following verbs are introduced in this lesson:

| VERB | MEANING | EXAMPLE |
|------|---------|---------|
| 1. Save | To keep what you did on a document in the computer so you can use it again later | I want to save this letter so I can remember what I wrote. |
| 2. Insert | To put a USB drive into the USB port of a computer | I have a document on this USB drive. I will insert it in the USB port so I can open the document I need. |
| 3. Increase | To make something bigger | I can't read the words. I'm going to increase the font size so they appear larger. |
| 4. Decrease | To make something smaller | The letters are too big, and the document is on two pages. Please decrease the font size so the document will fit on one page. |
| 5. Align | To bring into line on one side or in the center | Most documents that we type are aligned on the left side of the page. |
| 6. Scroll | To move the contents of a window up, down, right, or left | When you use the font menu, you have to scroll down to find the font that you like. |
| 7. Highlight | To click at the beginning of a letter and drag the mouse to the end of what you want to change | To change the text of this sentence, you have to highlight it first. |
| 8. Format (font) | To pick the font you want and use it in your document | I don't like the font on that letter, so I am going to format it with a new font style. |
| 9. Right-click | To press and release the right mouse button | You usually left-click the mouse button, but sometimes you have to right-click it. |

# Concepts and Exercises

CONCEPT 5.1 **Highlighting Text**

To change the format of text, you must highlight it first. You can see that text is highlighted when the background becomes black, as shown in the following figure.

**A.** Text Not Highlighted        **B.** Text Highlighted

> It is fun to change the format of my text. It makes my work look better. **Formatting also makes my words more interesting and easy to read. I can show which words are important.**

**HOW TO HIGHLIGHT TEXT**

Steps A–C show one way to highlight text, by dragging with the mouse.

**A.** Click at the right end of the text that you want to highlight.

> It is fun to change the format of my text. It makes my work look better. Formatting also makes my words more interesting and easy to read. I can show which words are important.

**B.** Hold the left mouse button down and move to the left and up, as you continue holding down the mouse button (dragging).

**C.** Let go of the mouse button when all the text is selected.

**HOW TO REMOVE HIGHLIGHTING**

Click anywhere away from the highlighted words to take off the highlighting

EXERCISE 5.1 **Highlight Text**

In this exercise, you will type some text in WordPad, and then drag with the mouse to highlight some of the text.

1. Open WordPad: Start→All Programs→Accessories→WordPad.

2. Type the following paragraph in WordPad:

   **It is fun to change the format of my text. It makes my work look better. Formatting also makes my words more interesting and easy to read. I can show which words are important.**

   Now you will highlight the first sentence.

3. Move your mouse pointer to the end of the first sentence.

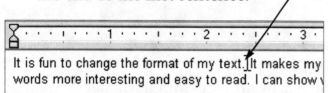

4. Hold the mouse button down and move to the left until the first sentence is highlighted.

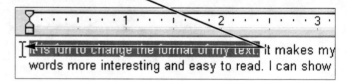

5. Let go of the mouse button.

   The first sentence should look like this. The highlighted text is also called a selection.

   > It is fun to change the format of my text. It makes my work look better. Formatting also makes my words more interesting and easy to read. I can show which words are important.

6. Click on a clear part of the WordPad window (away from the highlight) to remove the highlight.

   Leave WordPad open. You will soon learn something new to do with a selection.

**Formatting Text**

Formatting is done to make the text that you type look better. One way you can make it look different is by changing the font style. Here are some examples of different font styles.

| Font Name | Example |
|---|---|
| Times New Roman | This text is formatted with the Times New Roman font. |
| Arial Black | **This text is formatted with the Arial Black font.** |
| French Script | *This text is formatted with the French Script font.* |
| Papyrus | This text is formatted with the Papyrus font. |

Fonts can be different sizes.

| 10 pt. | 12 pt. | 18 pt. | 24 pt. | 36 pt. |
|---|---|---|---|---|
| ABC | ABC | ABC | ABC | ABC |

Here are some other ways to format text:

| Normal | Bold | Italics | Underline |
|---|---|---|---|
| ABC | **ABC** | *ABC* | <u>ABC</u> |

To change the format of any text, you must highlight it first.

## Font Dialog Box

One way to format text you have highlighted is to use the Font dialog box. Some features of WordPad's font dialog box are shown here:

**A. Font Box** – Click the font name to change the font type.

**B. Scroll Arrow** – Click on this arrow to see more font types.

**C. Font Style Box** – Click regular, bold, or italic here.

**D. Size Box** – Click a number to change your text to a different size.

**E. Sample Box** – This box shows what the text will look like.

**F. OK Button** – Click this button when you are finished.

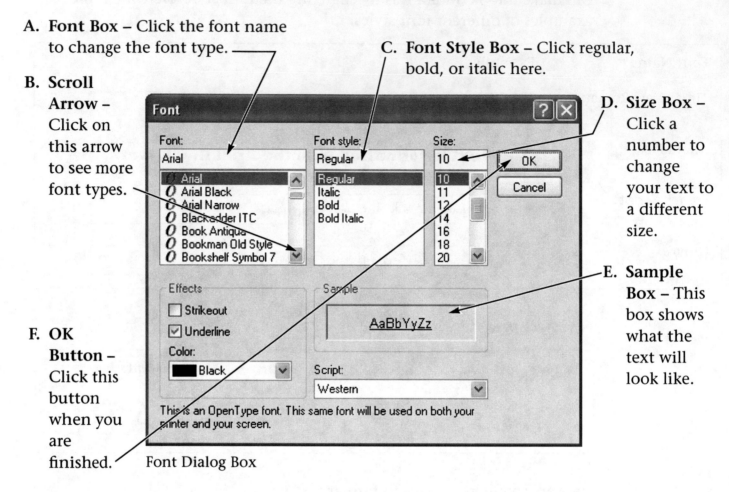

Font Dialog Box

EXERCISE 5.2 **Format Text in WordPad**

In this exercise, you will highlight text and apply a font format to it.

1. Highlight "fun" in the first sentence, as in the picture.

2. Click Format→Font on the menu bar to show the font dialog box.

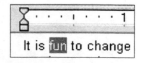

3. Click Arial Black in the Font box.

4. Click the down arrow on the scroll bar to see more fonts. Click the font types one at a time and look at the preview change in the Sample box.

5. Click Bold in the Style box.

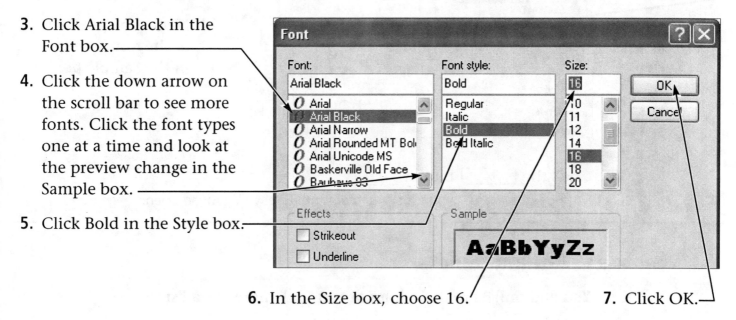

6. In the Size box, choose 16.        7. Click OK.

8. Highlight "work" in the second sentence on the first line.

9. Click Format→Font on the menu bar.

Now you will change the font format of the highlighted word.

**10.** Click the scroll arrow until you see Courier New in the list.

**11.** Click the Courier New font.

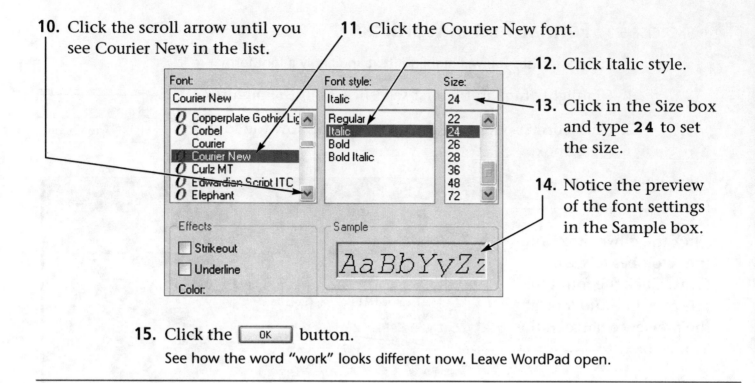

**12.** Click Italic style.

**13.** Click in the Size box and type **24** to set the size.

**14.** Notice the preview of the font settings in the Sample box.

**15.** Click the [ OK ] button.

See how the word "work" looks different now. Leave WordPad open.

---

CONCEPT 5.3 **Adding Bullets**

You add bullets to make lines of text look more like a list.

| |
|---|
| Days of the Week<br>Sunday<br>Monday<br>Tuesday<br>Wednesday<br>Thursday<br>Friday<br>Saturday |

**Without Bullets**

| |
|---|
| Days of the Week<br>• Sunday<br>• Monday<br>• Tuesday<br>• Wednesday<br>• Thursday<br>• Friday<br>• Saturday |

**With Bullets**

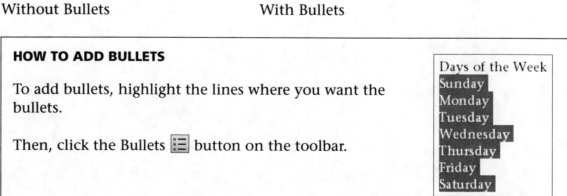

**HOW TO ADD BULLETS**

To add bullets, highlight the lines where you want the bullets.

Then, click the Bullets ⊞ button on the toolbar.

EXERCISE 5.3  **Add Bullets to a List**

In this exercise, you will type a new list and apply bullets to it.

**1.** Click with your mouse at the very end of the last line of text.

**2.** Press the ⌞Enter⌟ key three times.
Now your screen should look like this.

Cursor

**3.** Type the first six months of the year, as shown here. Press ⌞Enter⌟ after each month.

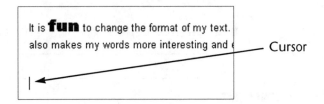

**January** ⌞Enter⌟
**February** ⌞Enter⌟
**March** ⌞Enter⌟
**April** ⌞Enter⌟
**May** ⌞Enter⌟
**June** ⌞Enter⌟

**4.** Highlight all the months.

**5.** Click the Bullets ⊟ button on the toolbar.

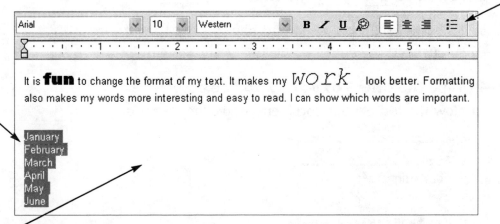

**6.** Click anywhere on a clear part of the screen to make the highlight disappear.

Now the list should look like this:

- January
- February
- March
- April
- May
- June

Leave WordPad open and continue with the lesson.

## CONCEPT 5.4  Changing the Alignment

You can use the buttons on the WordPad toolbar to change the alignment of a line. WordPad lets you choose three kinds of alignment.

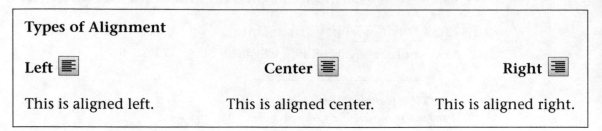

**Types of Alignment**

Left                               Center                           Right

This is aligned left.        This is aligned center.        This is aligned right.

---

**HOW TO CHANGE THE ALIGNMENT**

- First, click somewhere in the line or paragraph you want to change.
- Then, click the button for the kind of alignment that you want.

 ## EXERCISE 5.4  Change the Alignment

In this exercise, you will create a title for your document and change its alignment to Center.

1. Use the mouse or arrow keys to go to the very top of your document.

2. Press the ⎡Enter⎤ key two times.

3. Use the up arrow key to go back to the top of the document.

4. Type the title: **Formatting Text**.

   Now the top of your document should look like this.

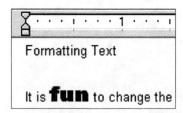

5. Click the Center alignment button on the toolbar.

   WordPad moves the title to the center of the screen. Leave WordPad open and continue with the lesson.

---

**Saving Your Work**

In the following exercises, you will save your work to a USB drive. Your teacher will tell you if you should save it somewhere else. When you save your work on a USB drive, you can move it from one computer to another. You can also take work you did earlier, open it on the computer, and add to it or change it.

In order to save work to a USB drive, you must first insert it into the USB port on the CPU.

---

**HOW TO INSERT A USB DRIVE INTO A USB PORT**

A. Find the USB port on the CPU. It can be on the front or back of the computer. Your teacher will tell you where to look on your computer.

B. Gently push the USB drive into the USB port. If it does not go into the port easily, turn it over and try it again.

C. You should be able to easily push it all the way in.

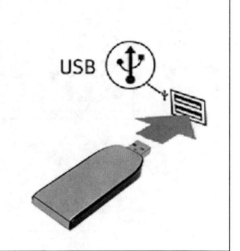

---

## Computer Files

When you save your work on the computer, it is saved in a package called a file. Each file must be given a name so you can find it again when you need it. Once you save work to a file, you can open it again later with the same program. The process of creating a file is called saving. Your screen may look different from the picture.

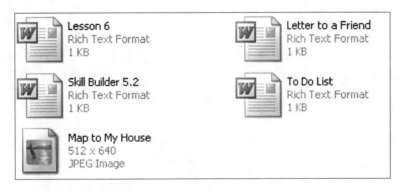

Examples of Computer Files

## HOW TO SAVE A FILE

**A.** Create some work in the computer program. For example, type a document in WordPad.

**B.** Click File→Save As on the menu bar.

**C.** Or click the Save ⊞ button on the toolbar.

**D.** Type the file name. You do not have to click there because it is already highlighted.

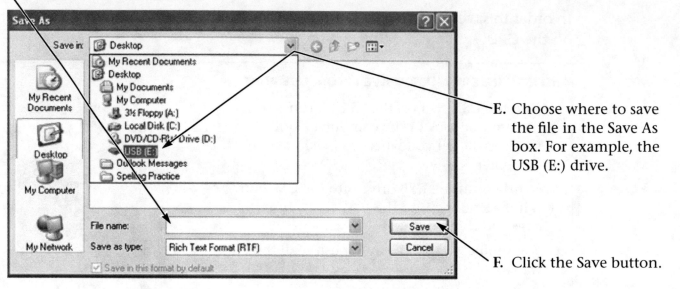

**E.** Choose where to save the file in the Save As box. For example, the USB (E:) drive.

**F.** Click the Save button.

After you finish your computer work, you must follow these steps to take out the USB drive.

**HOW TO SAFELY TAKE OUT A USB DRIVE**

A. Right-click the USB icon on the bottom-right side of the screen.

B. From the pop-up menu on the left, click Safely Remove Hardware.

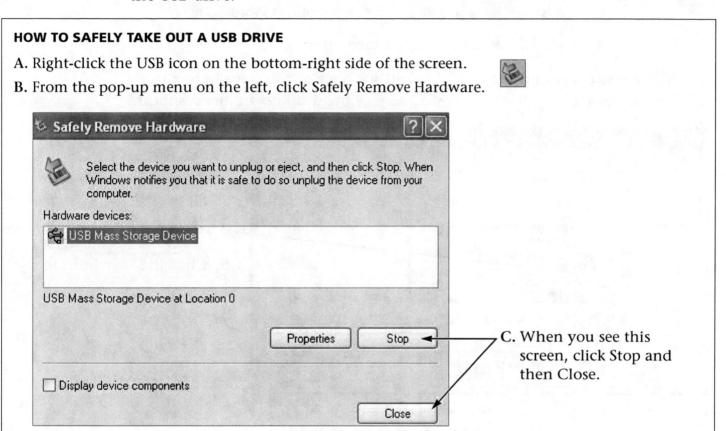

C. When you see this screen, click Stop and then Close.

D. When the computer tells you that it is safe to remove your hardware, you can pull your USB drive out of the USB port.

**EXERCISE 5.5 Save a WordPad File**

In this exercise, you will save the work that is in WordPad now.

**1.** Click File→Save As on the menu bar.

**2.** Type **Lesson 5** in the File Name box.

**3.** Click once on the Save In box to make the drop-down menu appear.

**4.** Click USB (E:) from the list. (Note: The USB drive letter and the name may be different.)

**5.** Click the Save button.

WordPad saves your work to the computer. Leave WordPad open.

# Skill Builder Exercises

SKILL BUILDER 5.1  **Change the Font**

In this exercise, you will practice changing fonts.

1. Open WordPad: Start→All Programs→Accessories→WordPad.

2. Type this paragraph. Do not press Enter until the very end.

   **I am learning to do many things on my computer. I am also learning new vocabulary words and verbs. I learned how to click on an arrow and look at the preview change in the Sample Box. I also learned to use the scroll bar to scroll to the size of font that I want to use. I plan to learn much more!**

3. Highlight the first sentence.

4. Change the font to Wide Latin, size 14, bold.

5. Click at the end of the first sentence. Press Enter.

6. Click in the middle of the first sentence and click the center align icon.

7. Save the file as **Learning**. (Save it in the USB [E:] drive or where your teacher tells you to.)

8. Click the Print button on the toolbar to print your work.

9. Close WordPad.

**Type a Bulleted List**

In this exercise, you will type a list with bullets.

**1.** Open WordPad: Start→All Programs→Accessories→WordPad.

**2.** Type the following words, pressing ⬚Enter where shown.

**Community Services** ⬚Enter
**Library** ⬚Enter
**Post Office** ⬚Enter
**Fire Department** ⬚Enter
**Police Department** ⬚Enter
**Parks and Recreation** ⬚Enter
**Public Health Department** ⬚Enter
**Department of Motor Vehicles** ⬚Enter

**3.** Highlight the first line.

**4.** Change the font to bold and any size and font type that you like.

**5.** Highlight all the lines of words except the top one.

**6.** Click the Bullets ▤ button on the toolbar.

**7.** Save the file as **Services**. (Save it in the USB [E:] drive or where your teacher tells you to.)

**8.** Print 🖫 your work and close ✕ WordPad.

**Change the Alignment**

In this exercise, you will practice changing the alignment of text.

1. Open WordPad: Start→All Programs→Accessories→WordPad.

2. Type the following words, pressing Enter where shown.

   ```
   Central Valley School  [Enter]
   1183 Riverside Drive  [Enter]
   Pleasant Hill, CA 94523  [Enter]
   [Enter]
   Dear Mr. Martinez:  [Enter]
   ```

3. Highlight the first line, and use the center ≣ button to center it.

4. Highlight the second and third lines, then right align ≣ them.

5. Highlight the last line, and left align ≣ it.

6. Save the file as **Central Valley**. (Save it in the USB [E:] drive or where your teacher tells you to.)

7. Print your work and close ☒ WordPad.

---

**Personal Project: Create a List**

In this exercise, you will create your own bulleted list.

1. Open WordPad: Start→All Programs→Accessories→WordPad.

2. Type a list of 10 cities in the United States.

3. Give each city a different font.

4. Highlight all the cities.

5. Click the Bullets ☷ button.

6. Save the file as **Cities**. (Save it in the USB [E:] drive or where your teacher tells you to.)

7. Print your work and close WordPad.

# Conversation

## Paired Conversation

With a partner, take turns reading the A and B parts of the conversation.

| | |
|---|---|
| Student A | Today's lesson is going to be fun. |
| Student B | Really? Why? |
| Student A | We are going to learn how to format our text. |
| Student B | I heard someone say that we will learn about fonts. |
| Student A | Yes, we will learn how to change our text. |
| Student B | That sounds like fun! |
| Student A | I know. We'll also learn how to make bold text. |
| Student B | That's good, but I like the way italic text looks better. |
| Student A | Well, we will learn both! |
| Student B | Did you bring your USB drive? |
| Student A | Yes, I did, but I don't know how to insert it in the computer. |
| Student B | I'll show you how to put it in the USB port. |
| Student A | Thanks. I don't want to mess it up. |
| Student B | We can put all this new stuff in our own documents. |
| Student A | Do you think we will be able to print today? |
| Student B | I think so. |
| Student A | We have a nice printer in the classroom. |
| Student B | Well, I'm going to be the first one to print my document! |

# Using the Internet

## LEARNING OBJECTIVES

After studying this lesson, you will be able to:

### Computer Objectives

- Open and use Internet Explorer
- Use a search engine to find information
- Type a URL to go to a website

### Language Objectives

- Use vocabulary words to describe opening and using Internet Explorer
- Describe actions to take when using a search engine
- Use appropriate verbs when describing how to find information
- Talk about typing addresses in the address bar
- Tell a partner how to go to a website

*Additional learning resources are available at **labpub.com/learn/esl/complit2xp/***

## Picture Dictionary

The following nouns are introduced in this lesson:

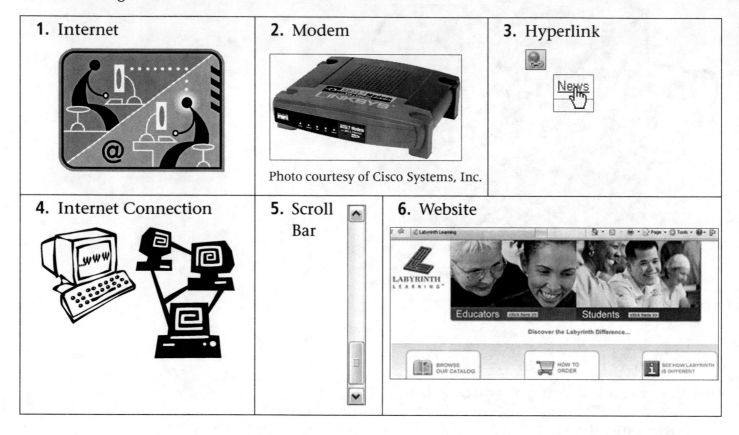

| 1. Internet | 2. Modem | 3. Hyperlink |
| --- | --- | --- |
| | Photo courtesy of Cisco Systems, Inc. | News |

| 4. Internet Connection | 5. Scroll Bar | 6. Website |
| --- | --- | --- |
| | | |

1. **Internet** – Computers from all over the world connected so they can communicate

2. **Modem** – A tool that connects your computer to the Internet

3. **Hyperlink** – An object or text that takes you from one web page to another when you click on it

4. **Internet Connection** – The system that lets you make contact with the Internet

5. **Scroll Bar** – The device that lets you move to other parts of a web page

6. **Website** – A place on the Internet where you can find information by using a search engine or URL

# Picture Dictionary (continued)

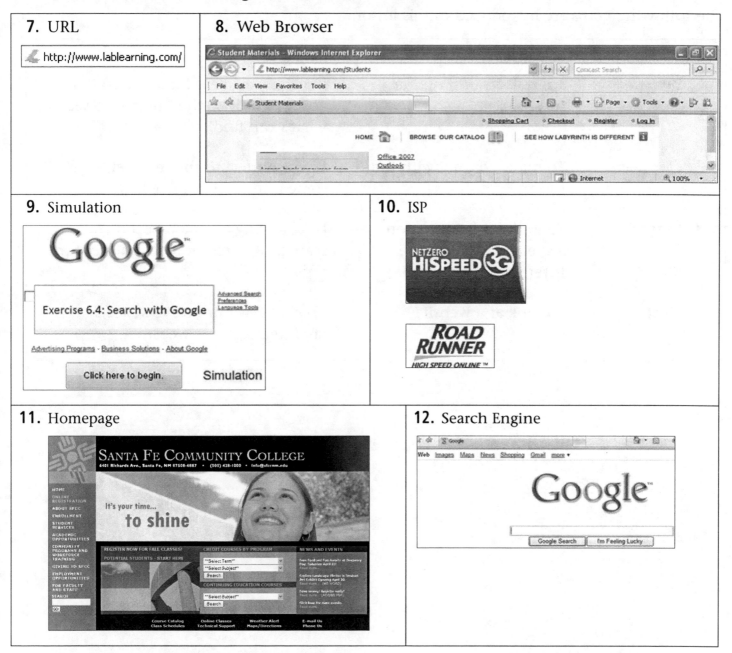

| 7. URL | 8. Web Browser |
|---|---|
| http://www.lablearning.com/ | Student Materials - Windows Internet Explorer |

| 9. Simulation | 10. ISP |
| 11. Homepage | 12. Search Engine |

7. **URL** – Uniform Resource Locator; the unique address for each web page

8. **Web Browser** – Software that lets you connect to the Internet

9. **Simulation** – An exercise that is not real. It is planned ahead of time, with all the possibilities already set

10. **ISP** – Internet service provider; a company that gives you a connection to the Internet, usually for a fee

11. **Homepage** – The page that appears when you open Internet Explorer or any web browser

12. **Search Engine** – A website you can use to look for things on the Internet

# Computer Verbs

The following verbs are introduced in this lesson:

| VERB | MEANING | EXAMPLE |
|---|---|---|
| 1. Browse | To look around on the Internet | I need some ideas for a gift, so I'm going to browse the Internet to see what I can find. |
| 2. Connect | To make contact with the Internet | I will connect to the Internet to get some information I need. |
| 3. Search | To look for information on a specific topic on the Internet | I am writing a book report. I will search the Internet for facts about my topic. |
| 4. Visit | To look at a website | I have a few minutes to visit my favorite magazine website. |

# Concepts and Exercises

CONCEPT 6.1  ## What Is the Internet?

The Internet is millions of computers from all parts of the world connected so they can communicate. To join the Internet, you must have an Internet connection. You get one by signing up with an Internet service provider (ISP). For most types of connections, you need a modem.

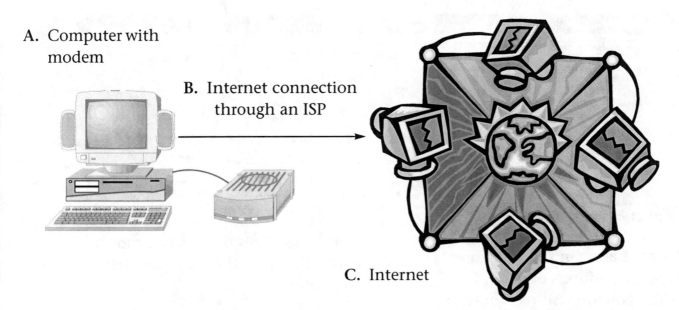

A. Computer with modem

B. Internet connection through an ISP

C. Internet

## Types of Internet Connections

There are a few different ways to connect to the Internet. They have different speeds and costs. For each type of connection, you should be able to find a few different ISPs in your area.

- **Dial-up** – This uses a regular telephone line to connect to the Internet. Dial-up costs less money than other types of connections. It is the slowest type of connection.

- **Cable** – This connection uses the same cable as cable television.

- **DSL** – You must have a special telephone line to use this type of connection.

- **Satellite** – A cable connects you to a satellite dish. The dish communicates with a satellite for Internet access.

- **Wi-Fi** – Wireless networking sends the Internet data through the air. No wires or cables are needed.

**Using Internet Explorer**

You need special software on your computer to connect to the Internet. That special software is called an Internet browser. Many people use Internet Explorer as their browser.

**A. Internet Explorer Title Bar** – This title bar tells you the website you are visiting.

**B. Menu** – Internet Explorer has a special menu for using the Internet.

**C. Toolbar** – Internet Explorer has a special toolbar for using the Internet.

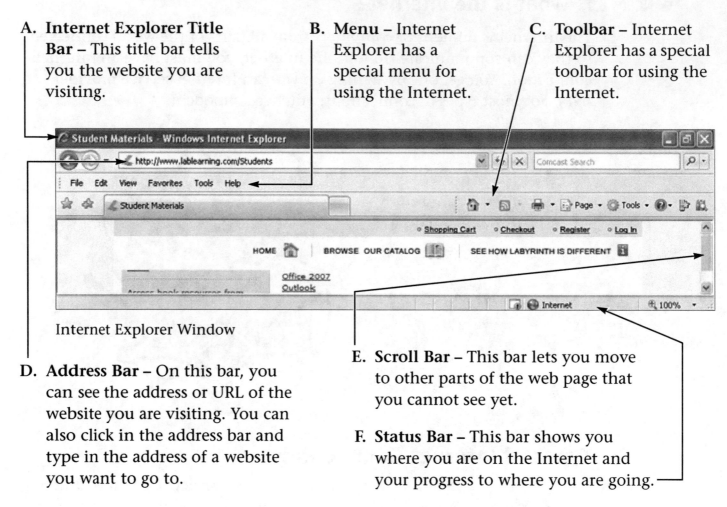

Internet Explorer Window

**D. Address Bar** – On this bar, you can see the address or URL of the website you are visiting. You can also click in the address bar and type in the address of a website you want to go to.

**E. Scroll Bar** – This bar lets you move to other parts of the web page that you cannot see yet.

**F. Status Bar** – This bar shows you where you are on the Internet and your progress to where you are going.

EXERCISE 6.2 **Start Internet Explorer**

In this exercise, you will start Internet Explorer.

**1.** Open Internet Explorer: Start→All Programs→Internet Explorer.

On some computers, you should look for Internet Explorer on the Desktop or somewhere else in the Start menu. Ask your teacher if you need help.

Internet Explorer Icon

The homepage will open. A homepage is the first page Internet Explorer shows when you start the program.

**2.** Point with your mouse (don't click) on the Back button. Watch for the screen tip to come up. ——————

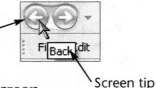

Screen tip

**3.** Put your mouse on other icons. Watch for the screen tip to show on each one. (The icons that have words showing do not have screen tips.)

Leave the Internet Explorer window open.

---

CONCEPT 6.3 **Using the Address Bar**

When you click in the address bar once, the address that is there becomes highlighted.

Then you can type in a new address. You do not have to use Backspace or Delete.

EXERCISE 6.3 **Go to a Website**

In this exercise, you will type an address in the address bar. Internet Explorer should still be open.

**1.** Click in the white part of the address bar and see that the address is highlighted.

**2.** Type in the new address, **yahoo.com**, and press Enter to go to the new website. —

**3.** Take a minute to look at this website.

**4.** Click the ⬅ button to go back to where you were when you started.

The place where you start when you open Internet Explorer is called the homepage.

CONCEPT 6.4 **Using a Search Engine**

A search engine is a website made to look for things on the Internet. Google is one of the many that you can use.

**A.** Name of the search engine.

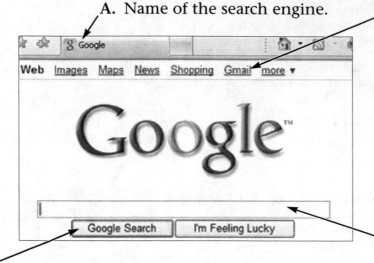

**B.** Links usually look like underlined words. When you click on them, you will go to another web page. You know that something is a link when you put your mouse on it and you see your mouse pointer change to a hand symbol 🖑. (The underlined word is the link and the mouse pointer is shown as a hand symbol on the link.)

**C.** Search box where you type what you are looking for.

**D.** Search button that you click to start the search.

EXERCISE 6.4 **Search with Google**

In this exercise, you will use a simulation of a search engine to practice finding information.

1. Start Internet Explorer if it is not already open.

2. Click once in the address bar. Type in this address:
**labpub.com/learn/esl/complit2xp**

3. Press the Enter key.
The website for this book appears.

4. Click the link for Exercise 6.4.
You will see a simulation of Google appear. Now you will do a search.

5. Click in the Search box and type **American flag**.

6. Click the Google Search button.

Google displays the search results. Notice how many there are.

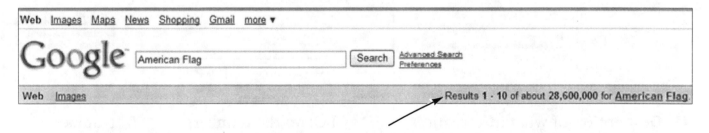

5. Click the button that reads "Click here to continue to Exercise 6.5."

**Search Results**

When the search engine gives you the results, take a few minutes to look at them. You have to decide which ones have what you are searching for. Sometimes you have to look at a few to get what you want. You can add more words to your search if you still cannot find what you are searching for.

**F.** Similar pages – click this link to see more results like this one

**G.** Sponsored links – sites that pay money to search engines to appear here, usually to sell something

**A.** Web page title

**B.** Web address or URL

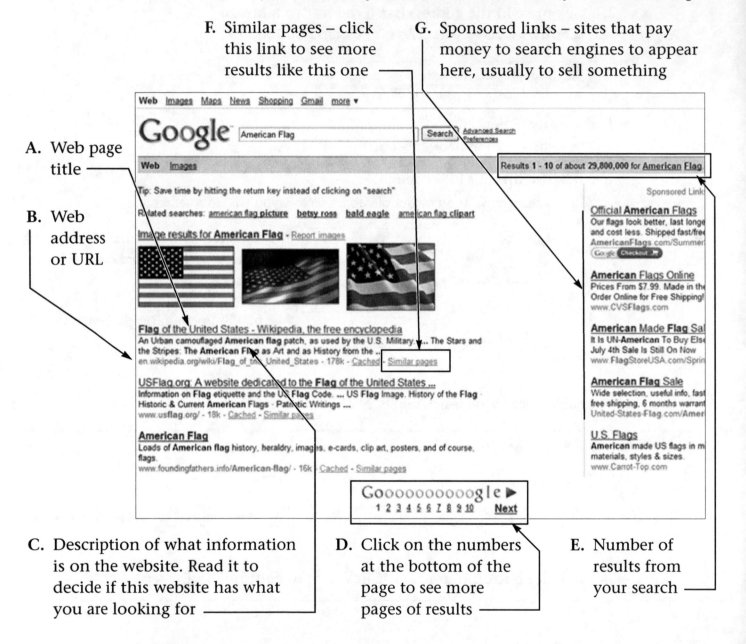

**C.** Description of what information is on the website. Read it to decide if this website has what you are looking for

**D.** Click on the numbers at the bottom of the page to see more pages of results

**E.** Number of results from your search

## Other Search Engines

These results are only from one search engine. They change every day and will look different when you use a different search engine, like Yahoo.com or Ask.com.

# Using Scroll Bars

Scroll bars are used to move around in a window. They let you go to parts of the web page that do not show because it is too tall or too wide to fit on one page. The scroll bars let you move around to see the rest of the web page.

A. Vertical scroll bar

B. Horizontal scroll bar

You cannot see the whole web page without scrolling.

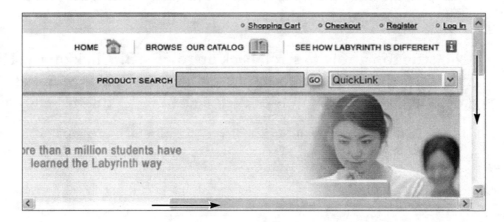

After using the vertical and horizontal scroll bars you can read the web page.

---

**HOW TO SCROLL THE SCREEN**

A. Click the bottom arrow of the vertical scroll bar to go down.

B. Click the top arrow of the vertical scroll bar to go up.

C. Click the right arrow of the horizontal scroll bar to move to the right.

D. Click the left arrow of the horizontal scroll bar to move to the left.

EXERCISE 6.5 **Go to a Search Result**

On the **Web**

In this exercise, you will use a simulation of a search engine to practice finding information.

**Before You Begin**: The Google.com search results should still be on the screen.

When you decide what link has the information you are looking for, click on its web page title.

### View a Search Result

1. Click the scroll bar to see more search results.

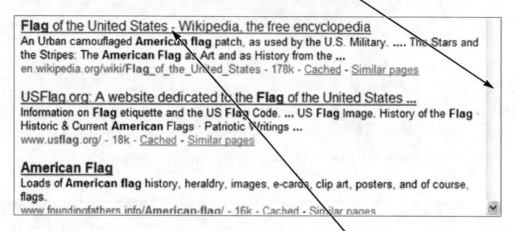

2. Click the top arrow to scroll back up to find the Wikipedia search result. (Wikipedia is a free online encyclopedia.)

3. Click on the Flag of the United States - Wikipedia, the free encyclopedia link.

The Wikipedia web page about the flag of the United States appears.

**Go to a Web Page Using a Link**

**4.** Point at the link for the 50 states, and notice how the mouse pointer turns into a hand. This tells you it is a link.

**Flag of the United States**

From Wikipedia, the free encyclopedia

*See also: Flags of the United States*

The **flag of the United States of America** consists of 13 equal horizontal stripes of red (top and bottom) alternating with white, with a blue rectangle in the canton bearing 50 small, white, five-pointed stars arranged in nine offset horizontal rows of six stars (top and bottom) alternating with rows of five stars. The 50 stars on the flag represent the 50 U.S. states and the 13 stripes represent the original Thirteen Colonies that rebelled against the British Crown and became the first states in the Union.[1] Nicknames for the flag

U.S. state

**5.** Click on the link for the 50 U.S. states.

You will see the 50 U.S. states web page appear.

**U.S. state**

From Wikipedia, the free encyclopedia

*"States of the Union" redirects here. For Brothers and Sisters episode, episodes.*

A **U.S. state** is any one of the fifty subnational entities of the United States federal government (four states use the official title of *commonwealth* rather t shared sovereignty, an American is a citizen both of the federal entity and of However, state citizenship is very flexible, and no government approval is req (with the exception of convicts on parole).

**6.** Click the Back ⬅ button two times to go back to the Google search results. Now you can look at other search results, or start a new search.

**7.** Click the Close ☒ button to close the simulation. Then, click the Close button to close Internet Explorer.

 # Skill Builder Exercises

**SKILL BUILDER 6.1** ## Go to Another Website

In this exercise, you will practice going to a website using the address bar.

1. Open Internet Explorer: Start→All Programs→Internet Explorer.

2. Click once in the address bar. Type answers.com and press Enter.

3. Click on any of the links that look interesting to you.
   Watch for the mouse pointer to change to the hand before you click.

4. Click the Back button to return to the homepage.

**Search the Internet**

In this exercise, you will practice doing a search on Google.com.

1. Click in the address bar. Type **www.google.com** and press Enter.

2. Click in the search box and type **US citizenship test questions**. Press Enter.

3. Look at the results that come up. Read the descriptions carefully.

4. Scroll down to see more search results.

5. Pick out one site you think has the information you are looking for, and click on its web page title.

6. When the web page opens, look to see if it shows what you want.

7. When you finish reading, click the Back button.

8. Try one of the other results by clicking on its title.

9. When you find a web page that shows one of the citizenship questions, print the page: File→Print.

## Fill Out a Form Online

1. Click once in the address bar. Type in this address:
   **labpub.com/learn/esl/complit2xp**

2. Press ⌷Enter⌷.
   The website for this book appears.

3. Click the link for Skill Builder 6.3.
   A web page appears with a simulated form to fill out.
   No information will actually be sent. This is just for practice.

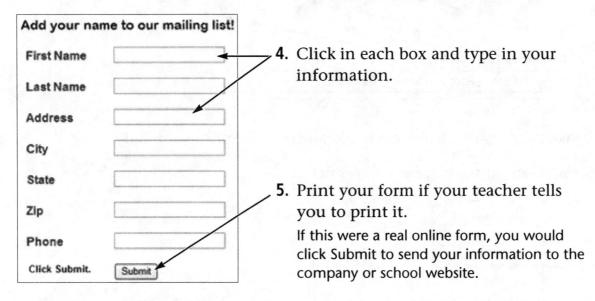

4. Click in each box and type in your information.

5. Print your form if your teacher tells you to print it.
   If this were a real online form, you would click Submit to send your information to the company or school website.

6. Close ⌧ Internet Explorer.

---

## Personal Project: Search for a State Governor

In this exercise, you will use the Google.com search engine to find information about someone in your state.

1. Use Google.com to search for information about the governor of the state where you live.

2. Click on some of the web page titles to see what information appears.

3. Print one of the pages about the governor using File→Print from the menu bar.

---

# Conversation

## Paired Conversation

With a partner, take turns reading the A and B parts of the conversation.

| | |
|---|---|
| Student A | I'm a new student. |
| Student B | Welcome to our classroom! |
| Student A | I heard that today's class is about the Internet. |
| Student B | That's right. |
| Student A | Which websites will we visit? |
| Student B | I'm not sure. We'll have to use a search engine. |
| Student A | Is that what you use to look for things on the Internet? |
| Student B | That's right. |
| Student A | Well, let's visit an interesting website. |
| Student B | I know! Let's go to our school's homepage first. |
| Student A | That's a great idea. Let's connect to it now. |
| Student B | Well, let's type in the URL for our school. |
| Student A | OK. Now what do I do? |
| Student B | We can use the hyperlinks to go to the pages we want. |
| Student A | Thanks. Now I want to browse the Internet. |
| Student B | You'll have to wait. We have to do a simulation exercise first. |
| Student A | OK. |
| Student B | Later, we can search for other interesting subjects. |

# Working with Email

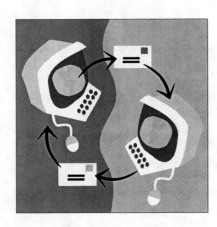

## LEARNING OBJECTIVES

After studying this lesson, you will be able to:

**Computer Objectives**

- Sign in to email and send a message
- Reply to an email message
- Forward a message

**Language Objectives**

- Use vocabulary words to describe signing in to email
- Use computer verbs to describe actions taken with email messages
- Describe how to reply to and forward a message

*Additional learning resources are available at **labpub.com/learn/esl/complit2xp/***

 # Vocabulary

## Picture Dictionary

The following nouns are introduced in this lesson:

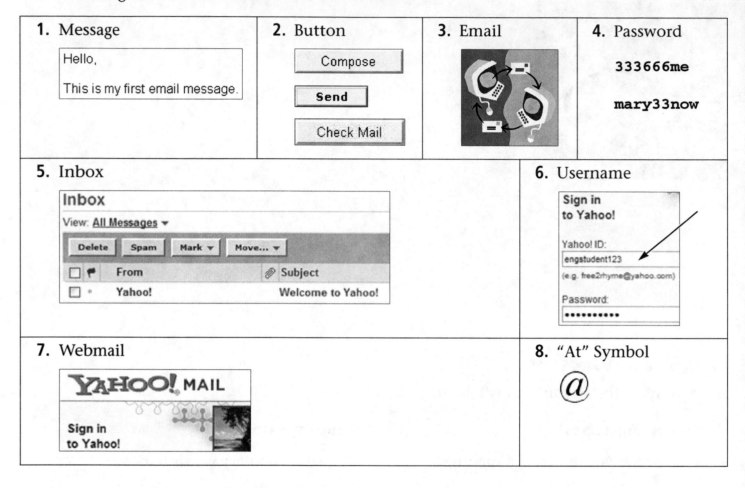

| 1. Message | 2. Button | 3. Email | 4. Password |
|---|---|---|---|
| Hello, | Compose | | 333666me |
| This is my first email message. | Send | | mary33now |
| | Check Mail | | |

**1. Message – Information that you type and send to another person by using email**

**2. Button – A small rectangle that completes an action when you click it**

**3. Email – Electronic mail; a way to send information from one computer to another**

**4. Password – A personal word or combination of letters and numbers that lets you go in to your email**

**5. Inbox – A page in your email that lists all the messages you have received**

**6. Username – The name you choose for your personal email account**

**7. Webmail – An email service that allows you to reach your email account from computers other than your own**

**8. "At" Symbol – The character that is included in email addresses between the username and the email provider name**

# Computer Verbs

The following verbs are introduced in this lesson:

| VERB | MEANING | EXAMPLE |
|------|---------|---------|
| **1.** Compose | To write a message | I'll compose a message explaining my absence and send it to my teacher. |
| **2.** Send | To transmit a message from your email to another person's email | I will send a message to my mother tomorrow. |
| **3.** Forward | To send a message that you received on to another person | I got a wonderful message from Mary. I am going to forward it to Jane, so she can read it too. |
| **4.** Reply | To answer a message that you received | I got a message from my friend that says that she is sick. I need to reply and ask her if she needs anything. |

# Concepts and Exercises

CONCEPT 7.1 **About Email**

Email is a fast and easy way to communicate to all places in the world that have the Internet. You must have an email address and Internet access to use email. All Internet service providers give you an email address when you sign up.

- An email address must have three parts. It cannot have any spaces.

Sample email address: student@msn.com

| USERNAME | AT SYMBOL | EMAIL SERVICE PROVIDER |
|---|---|---|
| student | @ | msn.com |

- You will be using webmail in this book. Webmail is useful because you can use it from any computer in the world that has Internet access.

- Many companies on the Internet offer free webmail. You can use a search engine to find the companies that do. One of the most used is Yahoo! Mail.

## Getting an Email Account

When you get an email account, you must pick a username and a password.

- The username is the special name that you use to access your email.

- The password must be entered to keep your email safe. No one can go in and read your email unless they have your username and your password.

After you get an email account, you can send and receive email.

EXERCISE 7.1 **Sign In to Email**

In this exercise, you will use a simulation to practice email before you try the real thing. Watch for buttons like "Click here to continue." You will have to click them to go on after you complete some of the steps.

1. Open Internet Explorer: Start→Internet.

   Now you will go to the web page for this book.

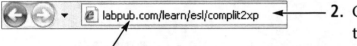

2. Click once in the address bar.

3. Type this URL and press ⌊Enter⌋.

4. Click the link for Exercise 7.1.

   You will see the Yahoo! simulation page.

5. Click the Mail link on the right side of the page.

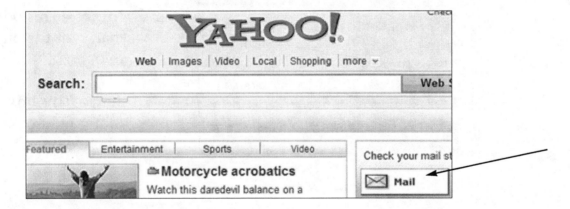

Now you will sign in.

**Sign In**

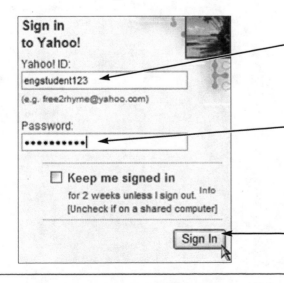

6. Click in the Yahoo! ID box and type **engstudent123** as your account name.

7. Type **learnmail** in the Password box. You will see dots instead of your password. This is to help keep your password secret.

8. Click the Sign In button.

CONCEPT 7.2 **Writing and Sending a Message**

Sending an email message is like writing a letter. You must add the email address of the person who will get the letter.

After you sign in to webmail, a window like this will come up.

**A. Contacts** – Clicking here takes you to your contact list, where you enter and keep addresses of people you want to send emails to.

**B. Compose** – You click here to write a new message.

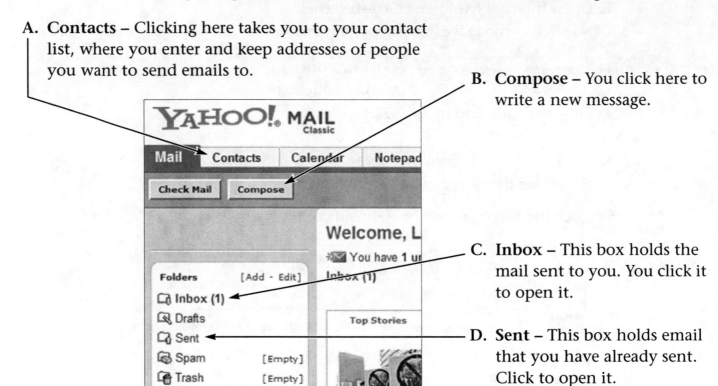

**C. Inbox** – This box holds the mail sent to you. You click it to open it.

**D. Sent** – This box holds email that you have already sent. Click to open it.

EXERCISE 7.2 **Write and Send an Email Message**

In this exercise, you will create (compose) a new email message and send it.

**Before You Begin**: You should be on the web page for Hands-On Exercise 7.2.

1. Click the Compose button.

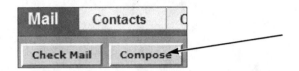

You will see a screen that lets you type a message.

2. Type the email address of the person you are sending it to in the To box.

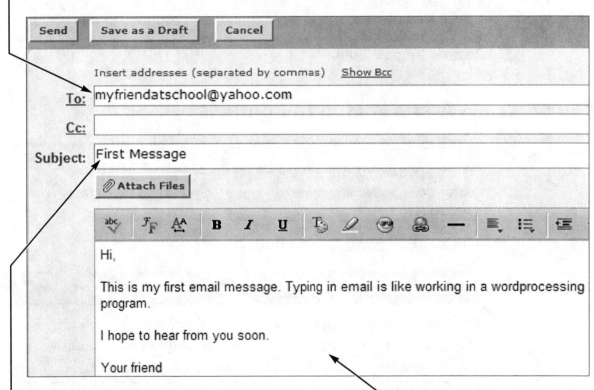

3. Click in the Subject box and type **First Message**. (This box tells what your message is about.)

4. Click in the message area and type the message shown here.

5. Click the **Send** button at the bottom of the web page.

The computer should tell you that the message was sent.

Leave the window open for the next exercise.

CONCEPT 7.3  **Contacts**

Contact Information is an address book with a list of names and email addresses. Yahoo! calls these names "Contacts." Yahoo! lets you save names and email addresses in your Contacts address book to use again later.

| Contact Information | |
|---|---|
| ☐ | **Armando**  [Edit]<br>armandishere@aol.com |
| ☐ | **Harry**  [Edit]<br>american1@msn.com |
| ☐ | **Janet**  [Edit]<br>thisisit@hotmail.com |
| ☐ | **Sandra**  [Edit]<br>sandra123@yahoo.com |
| ☐ | **Sergio**  [Edit]<br>computers4u@yahoo.com |
| ☐ | **Vanessa**  [Edit]<br>number1girl@earthlink.com |

Yahoo! Address Book

EXERCISE 7.3  **Add a Person to Contacts**

 In this exercise, you will add someone who just sent you a message to Contacts.

**Before You Begin:** You should be on the Exercise 7.3 web page.

Now you will save an address so you do not have to type it again for future email messages.

**1.** Click the [ Add to Contacts ] button.

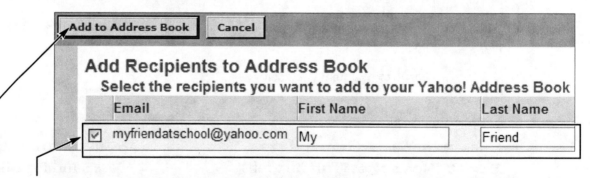

**Add to Address Book**  **Cancel**

## Add Recipients to Address Book
### Select the recipients you want to add to your Yahoo! Address Book

| Email | First Name | Last Name |
|---|---|---|
| ☑ myfriendatschool@yahoo.com | My | Friend |

**2.** Click in each box and type the information as shown here.

**3.** Click Add to Address Book near the bottom-left part of the screen.

You are now back at the main Yahoo! email page. Let's look at what you sent.

**4.** To see that you have sent the email, click on Sent on the left side of the Folders window.

**5.** Click the subject of the message to read it.

---

CONCEPT 7.4 **Reading Your Email**

Once you receive an email and open it, look at all the information it has.

A. The date and time the email was sent ————

B. The email address of the person who sent the message —

C. Your email address —

D. The message ——►

EXERCISE 7.4  **Check for New Email**

In this exercise, you will check your mail, open a message, and then print the message.

**Before You Begin:** You should be on the Exercise 7.4 web page.

**1.** Click [ Check Mail ] to check your email.

A new email message appears in the list.

**2.** Look at the name of the person who sent the message.

**3.** Look at the date the message was sent. (If no date is shown, then it was sent today.)

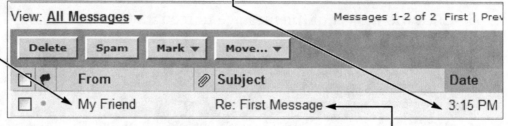

**4.** Click the subject of the first message to read it.

The message appears on the screen.

**5.** If you want to print the message, you must hold the [Ctrl] key down and press [P]. Then, click OK or Print. You must print this way because this is a simulation.

Leave the message open on the screen.

## CONCEPT 7.5  Replying to a Message

When you want to answer a message, you reply to it.

Reply | When you click the Reply button, Yahoo! takes you to the Compose window. You will see your cursor blinking at the top of the message box.

A. You type the answer to the message above the message.

B. You can use the scroll bar to see the rest of the original message.

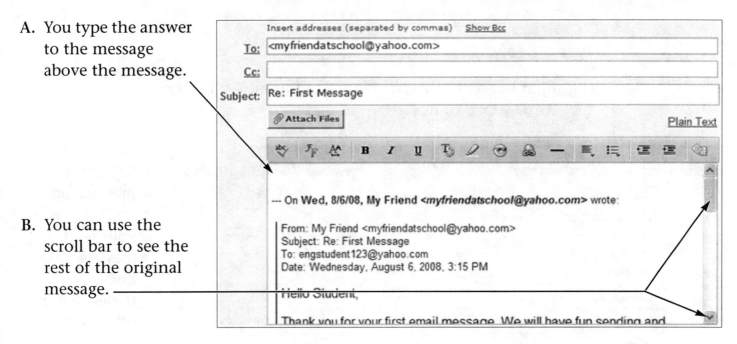

EXERCISE 7.5 **Reply to an Email Message**

**On the Web** In this exercise, you will send a reply to the email message you just opened.

**Before You Begin:** You should be on the Exercise 7.5 web page.

**1.** Click [ Reply ] to answer the message.

The Compose window opens for you to type your answer.

### Type a Reply

**2.** Highlight the text RE: First Message in the Subject box and type **Replying** to replace the old text.

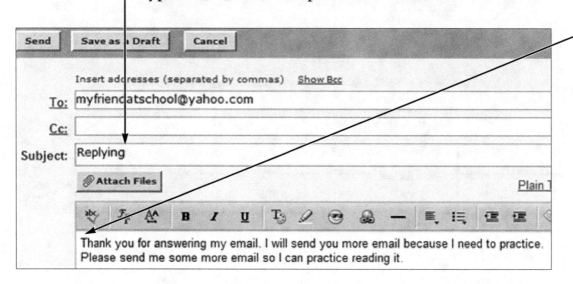

**3.** Click at the top of the message box and type in your reply message. It is not necessary to delete the other text.

**4.** Click the [ Send ] button at the bottom of the web page.

Yahoo! Mail shows that your message was sent.

**5.** Close ☒ the simulation window.

# Skill Builder Exercises

**Compose a New Message**

 In this exercise, you will write a new email message and send it. Remember that this is a simulation.

1. Open Internet Explorer: Start→Internet Explorer.

2. Click in the address bar. Type **labpub.com/learn/esl/complit2xp** and press Enter.
   The web page for this book appears.

3. Click the Skill Builder 7.1 link (hyperlink).
   You will see a simulated Yahoo! Mail web page.

4. Click the Mail button near the right of the web page.
   Yahoo! Mail shows a screen where you sign in to email.

5. Type this Yahoo ID and Password in the proper boxes.
   Yahoo! ID: **engstudent123**
   Password: **learnemail**

6. Then, click the Sign In button.

7. Click the [ Compose ] button below the Mail tab.
   A new message appears on the screen.

8. Click in the To box and type **myfriendatschool@yahoo.com** as the address.

9. Click in the Subject box and type **My Favorite Restaurant** as the subject of the message.

10. Click in the message screen and type a message about your favorite restaurant, with two sentences about why you liked it.

11. Send the message using the  button at the bottom of the page.
    Yahoo! Mail will show you a message telling you that your message was sent.

12. Click the Back to Inbox link.

13. Click the Sent folder in the folders box on the left side of the window.

14. Click the My Favorite Restaurant link in the Sent folder.
    Yahoo! Mail will show your message.

15. Click the continue to Skill Builder 7.2 button.
    This takes you to the start of the next exercise.

---

SKILL BUILDER 7.2  **Check for New Email and Reply to an Email**

In this exercise, you will check for new email and reply to a new email message.
**Before You Begin**: The Skill Builder 7.2 web page should be showing.

### Check for Incoming Messages

1. Click the [Check Mail] button in the upper-left corner of the web page.

2. Click the My Favorite Restaurant link at the top of the Inbox message list.
   The reply to your Your Favorite Restaurant message appears.

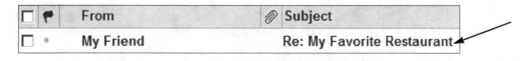

"Re:" means that this is a reply to the email that you sent.

## Reply to a Message

3. Click the [ Reply ] button at the top of the message. See that the To box and subject are already filled in for you.

4. Write a reply to the message describing your favorite car.

5. Click in the Subject box. Type **My Favorite Car**. Now the subject should read *My Favorite Car*.

6. Click in the Message box. Type a short message about your favorite car.

7. Click the [ Send ] button.

## Check for New Messages

8. Click the [ Check Mail ] button in the upper-left corner of the web page.

9. Click the link to the response to your message in the Inbox.

10. Click the Inbox link on the left side of the web page when you are finished reading.

11. Click the continue to Skill Builder 7.3 button.

## SKILL BUILDER 7.3 Forward a Message

 Sometimes you will want to send an email message that you received on to someone else. In this exercise, you will forward a message.

**Before You Begin:** The Skill Builder 7.3 web page should be showing.

1. Click the Inbox link in the Folders list on the left side of the web page.

2. Click the Welcome to Yahoo! Mail link at the bottom of the inbox message list.

3. Click the [ Forward ] button near the top of the message.

4. In the To box, type the email address **computers4uuu@yahoo.com**.

5. Click at the top of the message box, then type the following message:

   `I thought you might find this list of features in Yahoo! Mail to be of interest.`
   `[Enter]`
   `[Enter]` `[Your Name]` `[Enter]`

6. Send the message using the [ **Send** ] button near the bottom of the page.

7. Click the Check Mail button to display the Inbox.

The left arrow shows that you replied to (answered) this email. ——

The right arrow shows that you forwarded (sent) this email to someone else.

8. Click on the subject of the message to open the reply. ———————

   "Re: Fw:" means that this is a reply to the message you forwarded.

   | 📎 Subject |
   | --- |
   | ► Re: Fw: Welcome to Yahoo! |

9. Click the Back to Messages link near the top of the message.

10. Close ☒ the simulation window.

**Personal Project: Sign Up for Webmail**

In this exercise, you will sign up for real webmail on Yahoo! It is free and will look like the simulations you have been using.

⚠️**NOTE!** The Yahoo! Mail website may not look exactly like the pictures on this page.

1. Open Internet Explorer. Click in the Address bar and type **www.yahoo.com**. Press Enter.

2. Click the Mail link.

3. On the right side of the window, click Sign Up.

Yahoo! displays a web page with a form where you can create a new webmail account.

In the following steps, you may have to ask your teacher or a friend for help if you do not understand what you should put in each box. The top of the form should look like this:

4. Type the information in each box. Continue filling in the boxes until you reach the "Just a couple more details" area near the bottom of the web page; then continue to step 5.

5. In the box, type the numbers or letters shown below it. Be sure to type capital letters if the picture shows capital letters.

6. Click the box next to the I Agree button to finish the email registration. If there is something that you did not complete, the computer will tell you, and you can fix the problem and continue to Yahoo! Mail.

Yahoo! will tell you that you have a new webmail account.

7. Write down your username and password because you will need them to sign in to your email.

8. When you use your new email, click Classic Mail near the top of the website and then Switch to Mail Classic so your email will look like the exercises in this lesson.

9. Now you can go to your email account or close Internet Explorer.

# Conversation

## Paired Conversation

With a partner, take turns reading the A and B parts of the conversation.

| | |
|---|---|
| Student A | Hi. What are you doing? |
| Student B | I'm writing a message to my friend in India. |
| Student A | Really? How will you send it? |
| Student B | I'll send it to him by email. |
| Student A | Is it easy to send an email all the way to India? |
| Student B | Sure it is. It's easy to reply, too. |
| Student A | I want to compose and send a message, but I don't have email. |
| Student B | Well, you can get a webmail account. |
| Student A | How much does it cost? |
| Student B | Sometimes webmail is free. |
| Student A | Really? Will you help me? |
| Student B | Sure. You need to choose the name you want to use. |
| Student A | Is that what a username is? Do I also need a password? |
| Student B | Yes, you do. |
| Student A | OK. Now tell me what an Inbox is. |
| Student B | My Inbox is on the screen now. It shows me a list of the email messages that I received. |

# Writing Letters in Microsoft Word

## LEARNING OBJECTIVES

After studying this lesson, you will be able to:

**Computer Objectives**

- Use Microsoft Word
- Write personal and business letters
- Use the Word Ribbon
- Check spelling

**Language Objectives**

- Use vocabulary words to describe personal and business letters
- Use computer verbs to describe letter writing
- Use computer language to talk about writing letters

*Additional learning resources are available at **labpub.com/learn/esl/complit2xp/***

 # Vocabulary

## Picture Dictionary

The following nouns are introduced in this lesson:

| 1. Office button | 2. Tab | 3. Group |
|---|---|---|
| | Home | Paragraph |

4. Word Ribbon

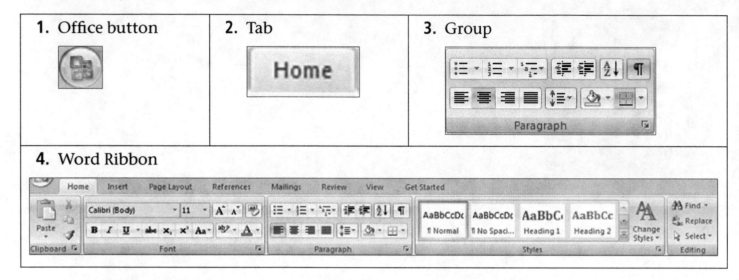

1. **Office Button** – The round, multicolored button at the top left of the Word window. It gives you options to open, save, or print a document. It also gives you other choices

2. **Tab** – A small rectangle on the Word Ribbon that you click to see different groups of buttons

3. **Group** – A set of several buttons that are together in a section under a tab

4. **Word Ribbon** – Composed of tabs and buttons grouped together

# Picture Dictionary (continued)

| 5. Quick Access Toolbar | 6. Spelling and Grammar Button | 7. ScreenTip | 8. Greeting | 9. Line Spacing Button |
|---|---|---|---|---|
|  | ABC<br>Spelling & Grammar | 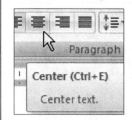 | Dear Maria,<br>My Dear Friend,<br>Dear John, |  |

| 10. Salutation | 11. Closing | 12. Complimentary Close |
|---|---|---|
| Dear Ms. Thompson:<br><br>Dear Governor Simpson:<br><br>Dear Principal Holtsman: | Sincerely,<br><br>Fondly,<br><br>With love and friendship, | Sincerely,<br><br>Respectfully,<br><br>With great appreciation, |

5. **Quick Access Toolbar** – The bar above the Word Ribbon and to the right of the Office Button. It has buttons that you use often

6. **Spelling and Grammar Button** – A special tool that will check your spelling and grammar in a document

7. **ScreenTip** – A little box that appears when you put your mouse (without clicking) on a button in the toolbar; it gives you information about the button

8. **Greeting** – The opening words for a personal letter

9. **Line Spacing Button** – A button in the Paragraph group of the Home tab of the Ribbon that is used to change the space between lines of text

10. **Salutation** – The opening words of a business letter

11. **Closing** – The last words before you sign a personal letter

12. **Complimentary Close** – The last words before you sign a business letter

# Computer Verbs

The following verbs are introduced in this lesson:

| VERB | MEANING | EXAMPLE |
|---|---|---|
| **1.** Open (a document) | To put a saved document on the screen | I need to open my document so I can make some changes. |
| **2.** Ignore | To pay no attention to something | I know I made a mistake, but I am going to ignore it for now and remember to fix it later. |
| **3.** Insert | To put in | Oh, I forgot to type my middle initial. I need to insert it between my first and last name. |
| **4.** Format | To make design choices about the way your document looks | Would you please help me format my document so it will look more interesting and professional? |
| **5.** Check spelling | To check typed documents to find incorrect spelling and grammar | I have many mistakes in my letter. I will check the spelling now and make the corrections. |

# Concepts and Exercises

CONCEPT 8.1 **Microsoft Word**

Microsoft Word is the most frequently used word processing program in the world. It does much more than WordPad.

---

**HOW TO START MICROSOFT WORD**

Start→All Programs→Microsoft Office→Microsoft Office Word 2007

---

You can open Microsoft Word from the Start Menu.

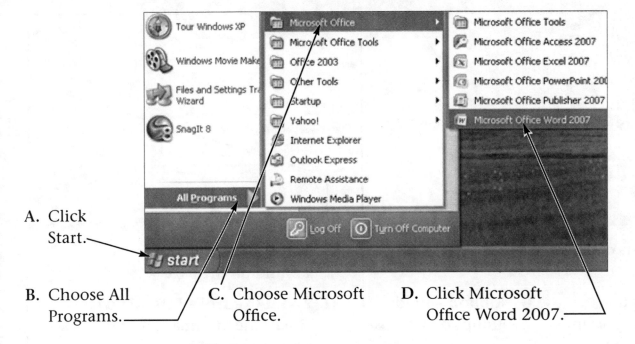

A. Click Start.

B. Choose All Programs.

C. Choose Microsoft Office.

D. Click Microsoft Office Word 2007.

Word opens on the screen.

 EXERCISE 8.1 **Open Microsoft Word**

In this exercise, you will open Word using the Start Menu.

1. Click Start→All Programs→Microsoft Office→Microsoft Office Word 2007.

2. Leave the Word window open and continue to the next page.

The picture below is the Word 2007 window. Look at the picture and try to recognize and name each part. This picture may look a little different from the one on your screen.

**A. Microsoft Office Button** – Click to open the menu

**B. Quick Access Toolbar** – Holds commands that are often used

**C. Title Bar** –Tells you the name of the program that you are using (it is always at the top of the window)

**D. Workspace** – Type your work here

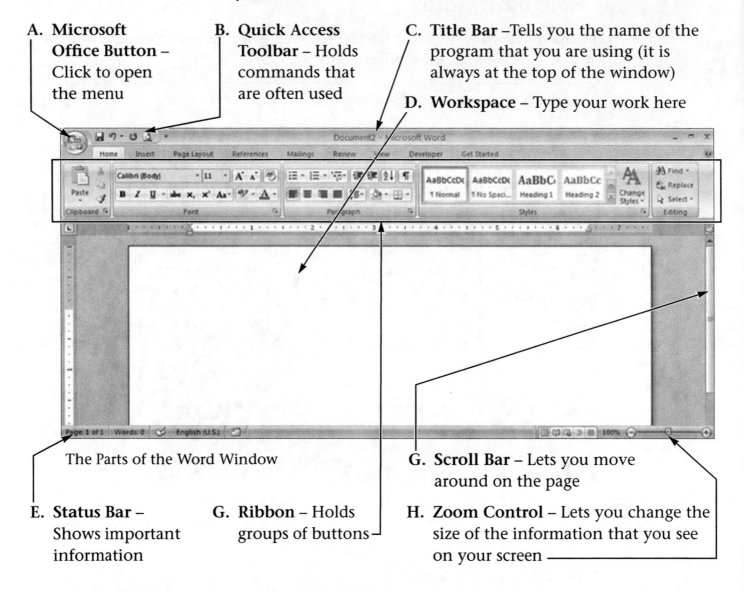

The Parts of the Word Window

**E. Status Bar** – Shows important information

**G. Ribbon** – Holds groups of buttons

**G. Scroll Bar** – Lets you move around on the page

**H. Zoom Control** – Lets you change the size of the information that you see on your screen

**A. Ribbon Tabs** – Click each one to use different groups of buttons

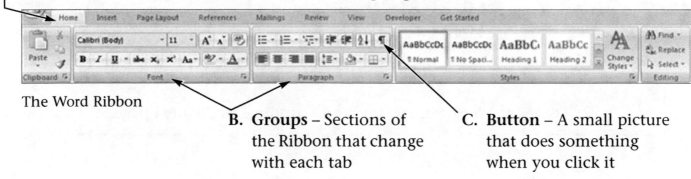

The Word Ribbon

**B. Groups** – Sections of the Ribbon that change with each tab

**C. Button** – A small picture that does something when you click it

The toolbars help you create documents and change how they look. ScreenTips tell you what the toolbar buttons do.

## The Quick Access Toolbar

The Quick Access Toolbar is a special toolbar on the title bar at the top of the window. It always shows and is easy to use. You can add or remove buttons from this toolbar so your Quick Access Toolbar may have different buttons.

A. **Save Button** – You click it when you want to save your work.

B. **Undo Button** – Click this when you want to cancel what you just did.

C. **Redo Button** – Click this button when you want to bring back what you just did.

Look at the button on the left that looks like a piece of paper. It is the New Blank Document button. That is one way to remember the Standard toolbar.

## ScreenTips

ScreenTips are little boxes that appear when you place your mouse pointer over each button. Every button has its own ScreenTip describing what happens when you click on it.

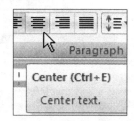

**EXERCISE 8.2** **Look at Word's Ribbon**

In this exercise, you will learn about the Word Ribbon and its parts.

1. Click the Review tab on the Word Ribbon near the top of the screen.

2. Find (don't click) the Spelling and Grammar button.

3. Click the Home tab.

4. Without clicking, put your mouse over each button and watch for the ScreenTips to show.

**Typing a Personal Letter**

A personal letter is a letter that you send to a friend or relative. It is not used for business.

**A. Heading** – This part has three lines: the name of the writer, the street address of the writer, and the city, state, and zip code of the writer. There are three blank lines after the heading.

**B. Date** – You must leave an empty line after the date.

**C. Greeting** – You put a comma after the name of the person you are writing to. You must leave an empty line after the greeting.

Melissa Jackson
1223 Appian Way
El Sobrante, CA 94803

October 23, 2009

Dear Jake,

I would like to congratulate you on your new job at the university. You have worked very hard to get this position. I am confident that you will do your very best and have a great deal of success.

I hope that you enjoy your new job and that your supervisor recognizes your talents and rewards you for your excellent work.

I know that you will work hard to be a good employee.

Sincerely,

*Melissa*

Melissa

**D. Body** – This is where you put what you want to say in the letter. You must leave an empty line after the body of the letter.

**E. Closing** – This tells the reader that it is the end of a letter. Put a comma after it. There are three blank lines to leave room for the signature.

**F. Signature** – Write your name here with a pen.

**G. Signature Line** – Type your name here.

## EXERCISE 8.3 **Type a Personal Letter**

In this exercise, you will practice typing a personal letter in Word. First you will change the line spacing so your screen matches the pictures in this book.

1. Click the Line Spacing menu button on the Home tab of the Word Ribbon.

2. Choose the 1.0 option.

3. Click the Line Spacing menu button again. (Step 2 closed the menu, so now you must reopen it.)

4. Choose Remove Space After Paragraph.

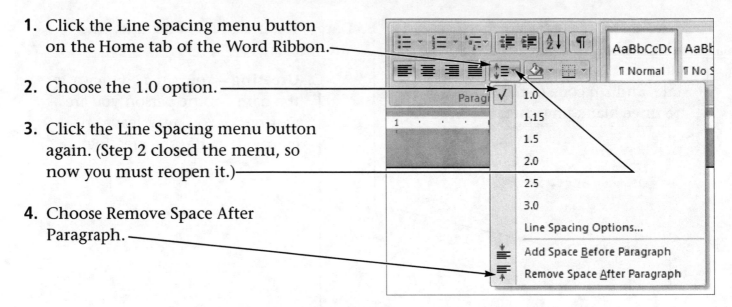

5. Type this letter and use the [Enter] key to add space between the lines.

   !**NOTE!** Your letter may not look exactly like the sample on the previous page.

<kbd>Enter</kbd>
<kbd>Enter</kbd>
<kbd>Enter</kbd>
**Melissa Jackson** <kbd>Enter</kbd>
**1223 Appian Way** <kbd>Enter</kbd>
**El Sobrante, CA 94803** <kbd>Enter</kbd>
<kbd>Enter</kbd>
<kbd>Enter</kbd>
<kbd>Enter</kbd>
**October 23, 2009** <kbd>Enter</kbd>
<kbd>Enter</kbd>
**Dear Jake,** <kbd>Enter</kbd>
<kbd>Enter</kbd>
**I would like to congratulate you on your new job at the university. You have worked very hard to get this position. I am confident that you will do your very best and have a great deal of success.** <kbd>Enter</kbd>
<kbd>Enter</kbd>
**I hope that you enjoy your new job and that your supervisor recognizes your talents and rewards you for your excellent work.** <kbd>Enter</kbd>
<kbd>Enter</kbd>
**Sincerely,** <kbd>Enter</kbd>
<kbd>Enter</kbd>
<kbd>Enter</kbd>
<kbd>Enter</kbd>
**Melissa** <kbd>Enter</kbd>

6. Use [image] Save As from the menu bar.

   The Save As dialog box appears, so you can save your letter.

**7.** Click the Save In drop-down arrow at the top of the Save As Window.

**8.** Click USB drive (E:), or choose a different place if your teacher tells you to.

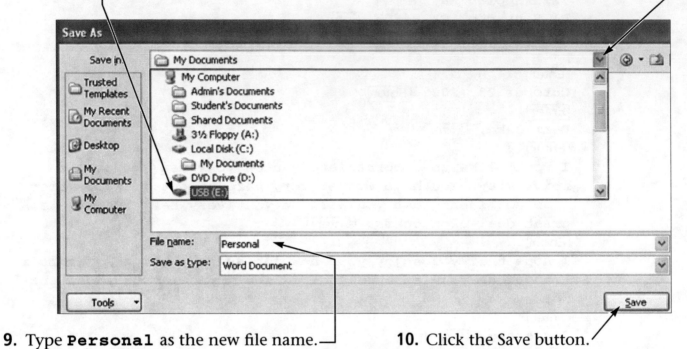

**9.** Type **Personal** as the new file name.

**10.** Click the Save button.

**11.** Look at the Word title bar. You should see the filename there.

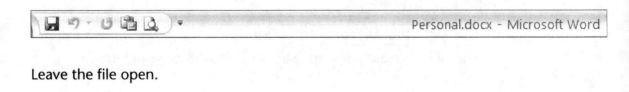

Leave the file open.

**Checking Your Spelling**

Spelling & Grammar

Microsoft Word comes with a special tool that will check your spelling and grammar. You will see this button when you click the Review tab of the Word Ribbon.

When you click the Spelling and Grammar button, a dialog box opens. It will show you which words you spelled incorrectly. In this book, we will only discuss spelling changes. You can learn about the Grammar changes, underlined in green, in a more advanced Word book.

A. Words not spelled correctly will appear in red. ——————

B. Word will give you some choices of spellings of the word. Click on the one you think is best. ——

C. Click the Change button if you want to change the word to the one you selected in the suggestions box. —

D. Click Ignore Once if you think the word in the document is spelled correctly. ——

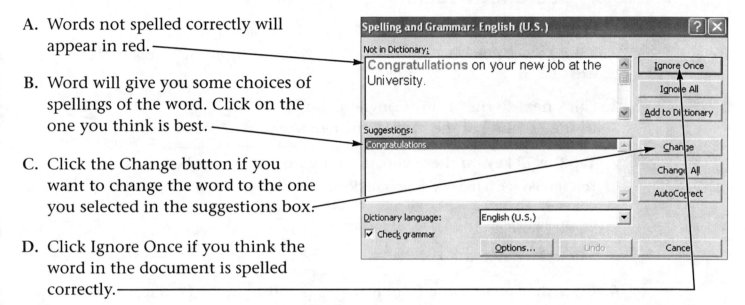

When Word is finished checking the spelling, this box will show.

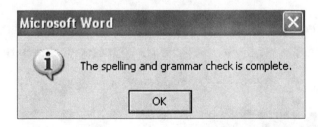

Click OK. Word also shows you misspelled words as you type. If you see a word with a wavy red underline, it means the word is not spelled correctly or the word is not in Microsoft's dictionary.

> Word is finihed

# The Spell Check Feature Is Not Always Correct

Sometimes the spell check feature can make a mistake, because it does not know the meaning of words. It would see both of these sentences as correct. But are they both correct?

- I red the book.

- I read the book.

 EXERCISE 8.4 **Use Check Spelling**

In this exercise, you will try the Spelling and Grammar command.

**Before You Begin:** Your document called "Personal" should still be open for this exercise.

1. Click next to the "l" in "Congratulations" in the first line of the body of the letter.

   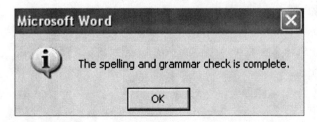

   Dear Jake,

   Congratulations on your new job

2. Tap the ⌺ key on the keyboard so the word is not spelled correctly.

   You should see a red line appear under the word to tell you that the word is not spelled correctly. Do not pay attention to any other colored lines now. We are only looking at red spelling lines.

3. Click the Review tab of the Word Ribbon.

4. Click the Spelling and Grammar  button in the Proofing group on the Ribbon.

5. Choose the correct word for any spelling mistakes in your letter.

6. Click the Ignore Once button if any green lines for grammar mistakes appear.

   The green grammar lines also show if you have more than one space between words.

7. When you are finished, this box will come up. Click OK.

   **Microsoft Word** ☒

   ⓘ The spelling and grammar check is complete.

   [ OK ]

8. Click the Save 🖫 button on the Quick Access Toolbar to save the file. Do not close it.

## CONCEPT 8.5  Typing a Business Letter

A business letter is different from a personal letter. A business letter is used to communicate with business people. It is often printed on special paper called letterhead, which has the business name and address printed at the top.

Here are the parts of a business letter:

**A. Date** – There are four lines inserted on the page before today's date is typed. There arethreelinesbeforethe inside address.

**B. Inside Address** – This is the name and address of the person receiving the letter. After the address, you must leave an empty line before the salutation.

**C. Salutation** – This part tells who the letter is to. After the person's name, you type a colon **:**. After the salutation, you must leave an empty line before the body.

**D. Body** – The main part of the letter tells what you want the letter to say. After the body, you must leave an empty line before the closing.

November 21, 2006

Ms. Juanita Thompson
Customer Service Representative
Urbana Software
810 Ivanhoe Way
Urbana, IL 61801

Dear Ms. Thompson:

I would like to thank you for your excellent customer service. You were patient and very helpful.

I have already used your software in my business. It has saved me time and money.

Please send me a list of the other software that you sell.

Sincerely,

Denise Smith
Small Business Owner

**F. Sender's Name** – The name and title of the sender.

**E. Complimentary Close** – This comes at the end of the body. The closing is followed by a comma. There are three lines before the sender's name.

## Starting a New Document

You start a new document by following the directions below.

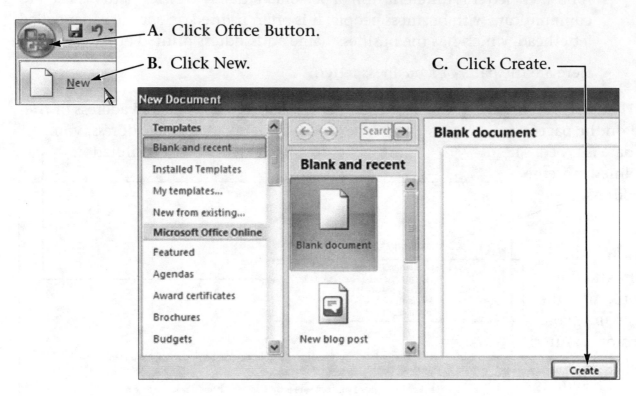

**A.** Click Office Button.

**B.** Click New.

**C.** Click Create.

EXERCISE 8.5 **Type a Business Letter**

In this exercise, you will type a business letter and then save it.

**1.** To create a new document, click ⬚→New→Create.
Word creates a new blank document.

**2.** Type this business letter. Do not worry if your lines end at different places than in the example.

[Enter]
[Enter]
[Enter]
[Enter]
[Enter]
[Enter]
November 21, 2006 [Enter]
[Enter]
[Enter]
[Enter]
Ms. Juanita Thompson [Enter]
Customer Service Representative [Enter]
Urbana Software [Enter]
810 Ivanhoe Way [Enter]
Urbana, IL 61801 [Enter]
[Enter]
Dear Ms. Thompson: [Enter]
[Enter]
I would like to thank you for the excellent manner in which you assisted me. You were helpful, informative, and very patient. You provided exceptional customer service. [Enter]
[Enter]
I have already used the software that you recommended. The software has been very helpful in my business. It has saved me a great deal of time and money. [Enter]
[Enter]
Please send me a list of other software that you carry and would recommend for my business. [Enter]
[Enter]
Sincerely, [Enter]
[Enter]
[Enter]
[Enter]
Denise Smith [Enter]
Small Business Owner [Enter]

3. Click the Save ![save icon] button on the Quick Access Toolbar and save the file as **Business**.

4. Close the file with ![office button] →Close.

**Opening a Saved File**

You save a file so you can open it later and use it again. This lets you work on the file without needing to retype it.

**HOW TO OPEN A SAVED FILE**

• You can open a saved file like this: 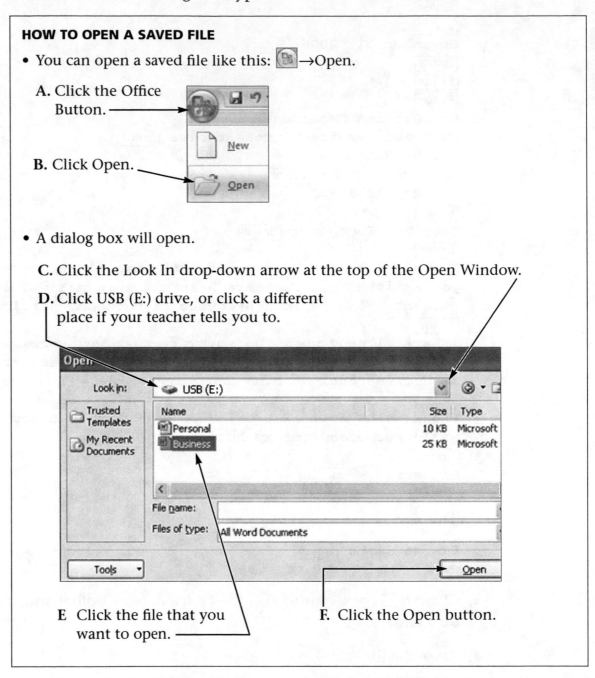→Open.

   **A.** Click the Office Button.

   **B.** Click Open.

• A dialog box will open.

   **C.** Click the Look In drop-down arrow at the top of the Open Window.

   **D.** Click USB (E:) drive, or click a different place if your teacher tells you to.

   **E** Click the file that you want to open.

   **F.** Click the Open button.

## Starting a New Document

You start a new document by following the directions below.

**A.** Click Office Button.

**B.** Click New.

**C.** Click Create.

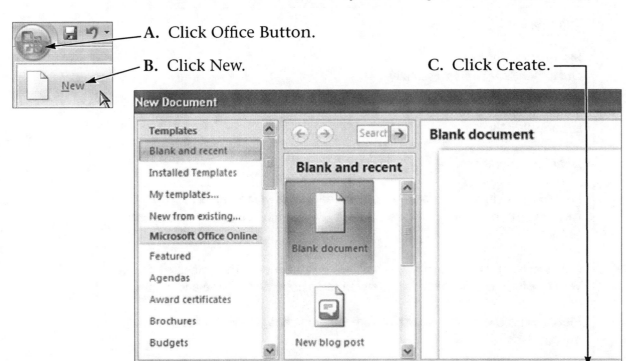

---

 EXERCISE 8.6 **Open and Print a File**

In this exercise, you will open and print the file that you saved in the last exercise. You will preview the document before you print it.

1. Open the Business file with 🖼️→Open.

2. Click the Look In drop-down arrow at the top of the Open window.

3. Click USB (E:) drive, or click a different place if your teacher tells you to.

4. Click the file that you want to open.

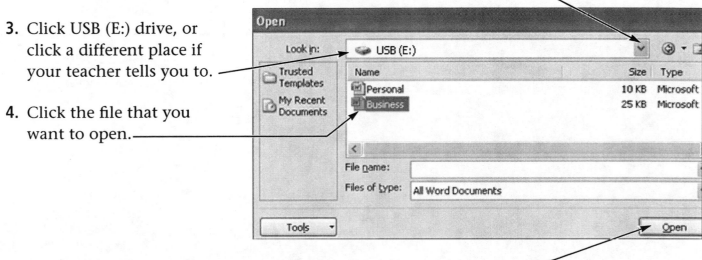

5. Click the Open button.

   Your business letter will appear.

**6.** Click →Print→Print Preview to see how the document will look when you print it.

---

June 16, 2009

Ms. Juanita Thompson
Customer Service Representative
Urbana Software
810 Ivanhoe Way
Urbana, IL 61801

Dear Ms. Thompson:

I would like to thank you for the excellent manner in which you assisted me. You were helpful, informative, and very patient. You provided exceptional customer service.

I have already used the software that you recommended. The software has been very helpful in my business. It has saved me a great deal of time and money.

Please send me a list of other software that you carry and would recommend for my business.

Sincerely,


Denise Smith
Small Business Owner

---

**6.** When you are finished looking at Print Preview, click the [Close Print Preview] button.

**7.** Print the document: Click →Print→Print→OK

**8.** Close ✕ Word.

# Skill Builder Exercises

**Type a Personal Letter**

In this exercise, you will type a personal letter.

1. Open Word: Start→All Programs→Microsoft Office→Microsoft Word 2007.

2. Type the following personal letter:

`Enter`
`Enter`
`Enter`
`Enter`
`Enter`
`Enter`
**Sam Carison** `Enter`
**345 Eastern Ave.** `Enter`
**Lodi, WI 53555** `Enter`
`Enter`
**October 10, 2009** `Enter`
`Enter`
`Enter`
`Enter`
**Dear Angela,** `Enter`
`Enter`
**I am planning a birthday party for Michael on Saturday, November 12th at noon. Can you believe that he will already be 10 years old? I hope that you and your family can make it. You don't have to worry about bringing anything. I will have everything ready for the party.** `Enter`
`Enter`
**Please call me to let me know if you and your family will be able to come to the party. Our telephone number is 209-555-6642. Try to let me know by Saturday, November 5th.** `Enter`
`Enter`
**I look forward to seeing you and your family.** `Enter`
`Enter`
**Please call me to let me know if you can come to the party.**
`Enter`
`Enter`
**Sincerely,** `Enter`
`Enter`
`Enter`
`Enter`
**Sam** `Enter`

**3.** Check the spelling using the Spelling and Grammar 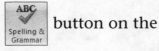 button on the Review tab of the Ribbonn.

- Change any words that are not spelled correctly.
- Do not change any of the names.

**4.** Save the file as **Party** using ⊞→Save As.

**5.** Click the Print Preview ⊡ button on the Standard toolbar.
Word shows what the document will look like when it prints.

**6.** After you look at the preview, click the [Close Print Preview] button.

**7.** Print the document using ⊞→Print→OK

**8.** Close the file using ⊞→Close.

---

SKILL BUILDER 8.2   **Type a Business Letter**

In this exercise, you will type and save a business letter.

**1.** To create a new document, click ⊞→New→Create.

**2.** Type this business letter:

**September 5, 2009** [Enter]
[Enter]
[Enter]
[Enter]
**Ms. Amelia Garcia** [Enter]
**Customer Service Manager** [Enter]
**Colonial Credit Corporation** [Enter]
**1000 Sherwood Place** [Enter]
**East Brunswick, NJ 08816** [Enter]
[Enter]
**Dear Ms. Garcia:** [Enter]
[Enter]

I have a credit card with your company. My credit card
number is 989-56437. My current credit limit is $4000. I
would like to have my credit limit raised to $5000 effective
immediately. ⌞Enter⌟
⌞Enter⌟
I have always paid my credit card bills on time. If you
review my payment history, you will notice that I have never
been late with a payment. ⌞Enter⌟
⌞Enter⌟
Please let me know as soon as possible if you will honor my
request. ⌞Enter⌟
⌞Enter⌟
Thank you for your help.⌞Enter⌟
⌞Enter⌟
Sincerely, ⌞Enter⌟
⌞Enter⌟
⌞Enter⌟
⌞Enter⌟
Your Name ⌞Enter⌟

3. Check the spelling using the Spelling and Grammar [ABC Spelling & Grammar] button on the
   Review tab of the Ribbon.

   - Decide whether to change or ignore what is
     shown in the dialog box.

   - Change any words that are not spelled correctly.

   - Do not change any of the names.

4. Save the file as **Credit** using [icon]→Save As.

5. Click the Print Preview [icon] button on the Quick Access Toolbar to see how
   the document will look when you print it.

6. After you look at the preview, click the [Close Print Preview] button.

7. Make any changes needed and save the file again.

8. Print the document using [icon]→Print→OK

9. Use [icon]→Close to close the document.

**Edit a Letter**

In this exercise, you will make changes to your saved Party letter.

1. Open 📂 the Party letter that you created in Skill Builder 8.1.

2. Make the changes shown in the picture below. Delete the words that are crossed out and add the written words.

---

*Joanna*

Dear Angela,

*March 30th*

~~I am~~ planning a birthday party for ~~Michael~~ on Saturday, ~~November 12th~~ at noon. Can you believe that ~~he~~ will already be ~~10~~ years old? I hope that you and your family can make it. ~~You don't have to worry about bringing anything.~~ I will have everything ready for the party.

*she*

*16*

Please call me to let me know if you and your family will be able to come to the party. Our telephone number is 209-537-6642. Try to let me know by ~~Saturday, November 5th~~.

*March 25th*

I look forward to seeing you and your family.

~~Please call me to let me know if you can come to the party.~~

Sincerely,

---

3. Print the document.

4. Use 📋→Save As to give the file a new name. Name the file **Party Letter for Joanna**.

5. Use 📋→Close to close the file.

**Personal Project: Type a Personal Letter**

In this exercise, you will type your own personal letter and save it.

1. Type a personal letter to a friend telling him or her about a new job that you will start soon.

2. When you finish typing, save the letter with the name **New Job**.

3. Print the letter after you save it.

4. Close the letter.

---

**Personal Project: Type a Business Letter**

In this exercise, you will type your own business letter and save it.

1. Type a business letter to a store where you like to shop. Explain what you like and don't like about its business.

2. When you finish typing, save the letter with the name of the store that the letter is about.

3. Print the letter after you save it.

4. Close the letter.

---

 # Conversation

## Paired Conversation

With a partner, take turns reading the A and B parts of the conversation.

| | |
|---|---|
| Student A | Hi! What's the matter? |
| Student B | I'm having trouble composing a letter to my grandma. |
| Student A | Why are you having trouble? |
| Student B | Well, I can't think of a good greeting. |
| Student A | How about "My Dearest Grandma"? |
| Student B | That sounds good! |
| Student A | Well, you don't want it to sound like a business letter! |
| Student B | That's true! |
| Student A | You should format your letter so it will look nice. |
| Student B | I know. I want a nice font. |
| Student A | You will need to use the Word Ribbon. |
| Student B | I only know a little bit about the Ribbon with all the groups of buttons. |
| Student A | You should also read the ScreenTips when they appear. |
| Student B | Yes, they help me a lot. |
| Student A | Have you thought about a closing? |
| Student B | I think I will write "Your Loving Granddaughter." |
| Student A | That sounds great. Don't forget to check your spelling! |
| Student B | I won't! |

# Copying and Pasting

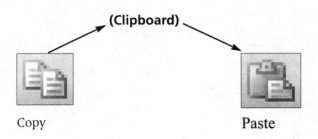

Copy       (Clipboard)       Paste

## LEARNING OBJECTIVES

After studying this lesson, you will be able to:

**Computer Objectives**

- Use Undo
- Use Copy and Paste
- Move from one open program to another

**Language Objectives**

- Use vocabulary words to describe how to copy and paste
- Use computer verbs to describe drag and drop and undo actions
- Talk with a partner about concepts introduced in this lesson

*Additional learning resources are available at **labpub.com/learn/esl/complit2xp/***

# Vocabulary

## Picture Dictionary

The following nouns are introduced in this lesson:

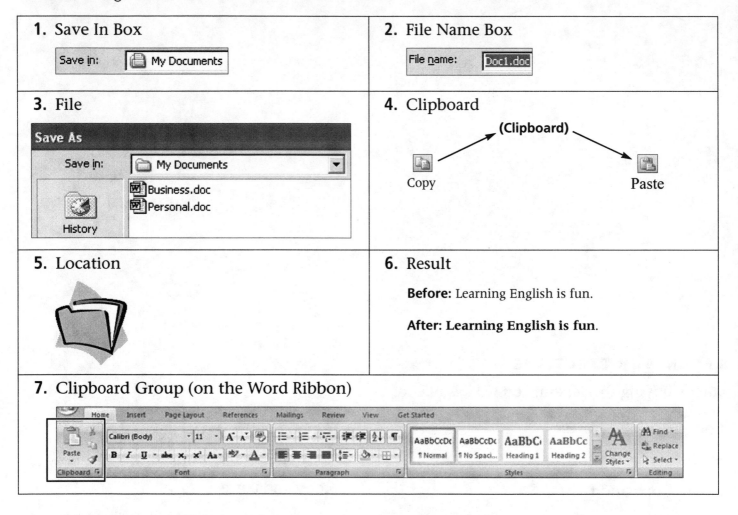

1. **Save In Box** – A box that allows you to choose where to save a document

2. **File Name Box** – A box that appears when you want to save a document that lets you type a document name

3. **File** – A piece of work, such as a letter or picture, that is saved in the computer; a file can also be part of a computer program

4. **Clipboard** – The place in the computer's memory where something goes when you copy it, before you paste it in a new location

5. **Location** – The place where something is

6. **Result** – The effect of a change you make

7. **Clipboard Group** – Part of the Home tab of the Word Ribbon that holds the Copy and Paste buttons

# Computer Verbs

The following verbs are introduced in this lesson:

| VERB | MEANING | EXAMPLE |
|------|---------|---------|
| 1. Cut | To take away or delete text or information that you do not want | I don't like that sentence. I am going to cut it from the story. |
| 2. Copy | To duplicate text in a document so you can put it in a different location | I will copy this sentence from Mr. Smith's letter so I can put it in Mr. Garcia's letter too. |
| 3. Paste | To take text that you copied and put it in a new location | I copied my address from the first letter. Now I will paste it into all the other letters. |
| 4. Move | To change the location of text or other information | My address is in the wrong place. I will move it so it is under my name. |
| 5. Undo | To cancel the last thing that you did | Oops, I made a mistake. I will just press the Undo button and undo it. |
| 6. Multitask | To do more than one thing at the same time | I will multitask and look at two programs at the same time. |

# **Concepts and Exercises**

**Copying and Pasting Within a Program**

Sometimes you want to repeat a word or sentence in a document. To save time, you can copy that information instead of typing it again. When you copy something, it goes to a place in the computer's memory that you cannot see, called the Clipboard. The computer keeps it there until you copy something else or close the program.

## **An Example of Copy and Paste**

These figures show how the Copy and Paste commands work.

**A.** You select (highlight) what you want to copy, and then you click the Copy 📋 button.

> Melissa Jackson
> 1223 Appian Way
> El Sobrante, CA 94803
>
>
> October 23, 2009
>
>
> Dear Jake,
>
> I would like to congratulate you on your new job at the university. You have worked very hard to get this position. I am confident that you will do your very best and have a great deal of success.
>
> I hope that you enjoy your new job and that your supervisor recognizes your talents and rewards you for your excellent work.

**B.** You click where you want to paste what you copied.

> I would like to congratulate you on your new job at the university. You have worked very hard to get this position. I am confident that you will do your very best and have a great deal of success.
>
> I hope that you enjoy your new job and that your supervisor recognizes your talents and rewards you for your excellent work. We look forward to seeing you at the family picnic in |

**C.** After you click the Paste 📋 button, the copied text appears.

> I hope that you enjoy your new job and that your supervisor recognizes your talents and rewards you for your excellent work. We look forward to seeing you at the family picnic in El Sobrante.

**HOW TO COPY AND PASTE**

- To copy information, you must highlight it first.
- Click the Copy button  on the Home tab of the Word Ribbon. You will not see anything happen yet. The information is now in a place in the computer called the Clipboard.
- Click where you want the information to go.
- Click the Paste button on the Home tab of the Word Ribbon to put the information into your document.
- If you see any other buttons appear automatically, do not click on them. They will go away as you do more work or after you save the file.
- The pasted information stays where it was and it also goes to the new location.

EXERCISE 9.1  **Open and Change a Letter File**

In this exercise, you will practice opening, changing, and saving a personal letter in Word.

1. Open Microsoft Word: Start→All Programs→Microsoft Office→Microsoft Office Word 2007.

2. Open the Personal file that you made in Lesson 8, Writing Letters in Microsoft Word. Use →Open.

3. Click here if you do not see your file and need to look somewhere else to find it.

4. Click on the file that you want to open.

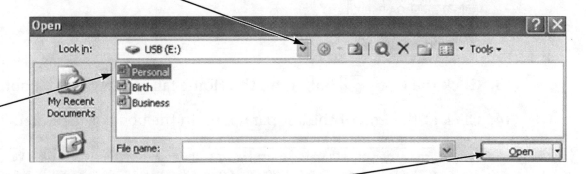

5. Click the Open button.

Word displays the document on the screen so you can work on it. Now you will change the line spacing so your screen matches the pictures in this book.

6. Highlight all of the letter. Start at the very top and hold the mouse button down until you reach the end of the last word at the bottom.

7. Click the Line Spacing menu button on the Home tab of the Word Ribbon.

8. Choose the 1.0 option.

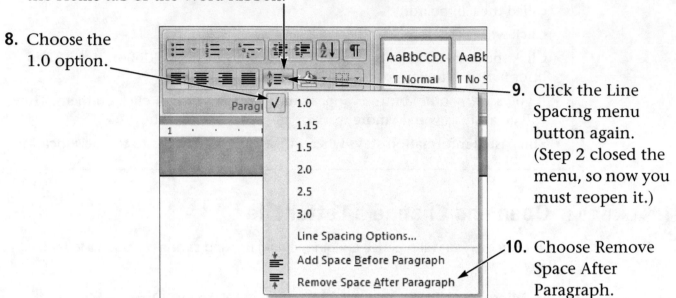

9. Click the Line Spacing menu button again. (Step 2 closed the menu, so now you must reopen it.)

10. Choose Remove Space After Paragraph.

11. Click the mouse in the empty white section of the window, away from the highlighted text.

12. Highlight "El Sobrante" near the top of the letter.

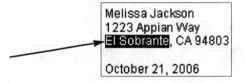

Melissa Jackson
1223 Appian Way
El Sobrante, CA 94803

October 21, 2006

13. Click the Copy button on the Home tab of the Word Ribbon.

14. Click at the end of the last paragraph in the body of the letter.

I would like to congratulate you on your new job at the university. You have worked very hard to get this position. I am confident that you will do your very best and have a great deal of success.

I hope that you enjoy your new job and that your supervisor recognizes your talents and rewards you for your excellent work. |

Sincerely,

15. Put in a space then type these words:

    We look forward to seeing you at the family picnic in

### Paste the Copied Address

**16.** Put in another space. Then, click the Paste 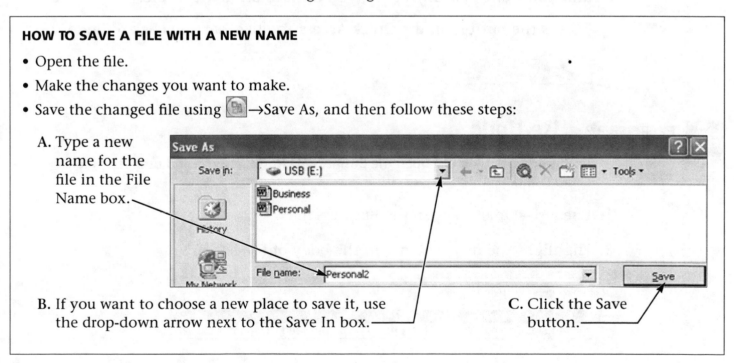 button to paste "El Sobrante" at the end of the sentence that you just typed.

**17.** Type a period to end the sentence. The changed paragraph should look like this:

> I hope that you enjoy your new job and that your supervisor recognizes your talents and rewards you for your excellent work. We look forward to seeing you at the family picnic in El Sobrante.
>
> Sincerely,

Word pastes the copied text into the new position. Do not close this document.

---

CONCEPT 9.2 **Saving a File with a New Name**

Sometimes you want to make changes to a file but still keep the old unchanged file. You can keep the old file under the old name and save the new file with the changes using a new name.

**HOW TO SAVE A FILE WITH A NEW NAME**

- Open the file.
- Make the changes you want to make.
- Save the changed file using [icon] →Save As, and then follow these steps:

A. Type a new name for the file in the File Name box.

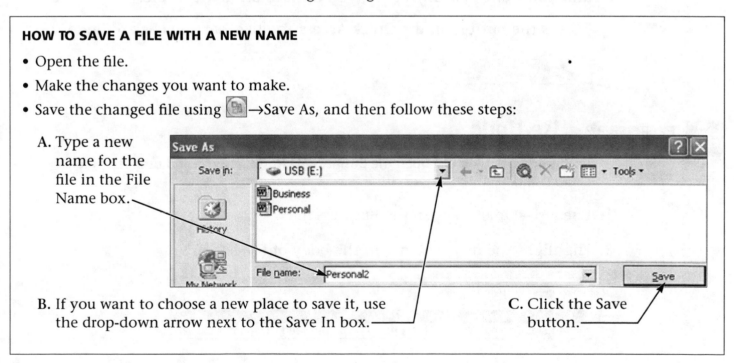

B. If you want to choose a new place to save it, use the drop-down arrow next to the Save In box.——

C. Click the Save button.——

**EXERCISE 9.2** **Change the File Name of a Letter**

In this exercise, you will make changes to the Personal document and save it with a different file name. That way you will keep the old file and have the new one too.

**1.** Highlight Melissa's name and address at the top of the letter.

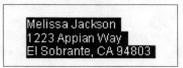

**2.** Press the Delete key to delete the highlighted area.

**3.** Save the file as **Personal2** using 📋→Save As.

**4.** Use 📋→Close to close the file.

---

**CONCEPT 9.3** **Using Undo**

↩ You use Undo to cancel the last thing you did. If you just deleted a word and you want to bring it back, you want to undo the delete.

This is the button on the Quick Access Toolbar that you click to undo.

**EXERCISE 9.3** **Use Undo**

In this exercise, you will open the Business file from Lesson 8 and use it to practice using Undo.

**1.** Use 📋→Open to open the Business file.

**2.** Highlight the first sentence in the body of the letter.

Dear Ms. Thompson:

were helpful, informative, and very patient. You provided exceptional custome

**3.** Click the Cut ✂ button in the Clipboard group.

The highlighted sentence should disappear.

**4.** Click the Undo ↩ button.

The sentence should appear again.

5. Click in the first line of the Complimentary Close between Sincerely and the comma.

6. Type a space and the word **Yours**.

7. Click the Undo button.

   The word that you just typed should go away.

8. Save the file using the Save button on the Quick Access Toolbar. Do not close it.

   This easily saves the file with the same name it had before.

9. Save the file as **Business2**. Do not close it.

CONCEPT 9.4 **Moving Text in Word**

The easiest way to move text is to highlight and drag it to a new place. It is different from copy and paste because the text does not stay where it was before. It is only in the new place. This is how it is done.

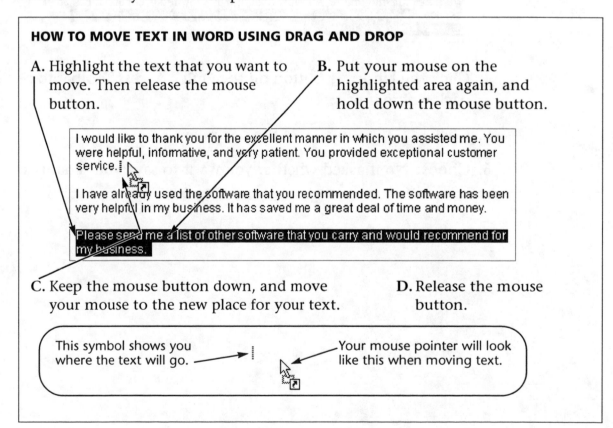

**HOW TO MOVE TEXT IN WORD USING DRAG AND DROP**

A. Highlight the text that you want to move. Then release the mouse button.

B. Put your mouse on the highlighted area again, and hold down the mouse button.

I would like to thank you for the excellent manner in which you assisted me. You were helpful, informative, and very patient. You provided exceptional customer service.

I have already used the software that you recommended. The software has been very helpful in my business. It has saved me a great deal of time and money.

Please send me a list of other software that you carry and would recommend for my business.

C. Keep the mouse button down, and move your mouse to the new place for your text.

D. Release the mouse button.

This symbol shows you where the text will go. ⟶

Your mouse pointer will look like this when moving text.

EXERCISE 9.4 **Move Text with Drag and Drop**

In this exercise, you will move the last sentence up to the first paragraph, and then undo the action.

**1.** Highlight the last sentence of the Business2 letter. Release the mouse button.

**2.** Put your mouse on the highlighted area again, and hold down the mouse button.

I would like to thank you for the excellent manner in which you assisted me. You were helpful, informative, and very patient. You provided exceptional customer service.

I have already used the software that you recommended. The software has been very helpful in my business. It has saved me a great deal of time and money.

Please send me a list of other software that you carry and would recommend for my business.

**3.** Drag the sentence to the end of the first paragraph of the letter. Release the mouse button.

See that the sentence is at the new location. It should look like the picture below:

I would like to thank you for the excellent manner in which you assisted me. You were helpful, informative, and very patient. You provided exceptional customer service. Please send me a list of other software that you carry and would recommend for my business.

**4.** Click the Undo button on the Quick Access Toolbar to put the sentence back where it was.

**5.** Click →Close to close the document.

**6.** Choose No if asked whether you want to save your changes.

**Using Right-Click to Copy and Paste**

Sometimes it is easier to copy and paste by clicking the right mouse button.

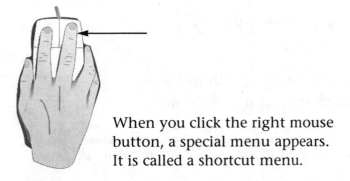

When you click the right mouse button, a special menu appears. It is called a shortcut menu.

---

**HOW TO COPY USING A RIGHT-CLICK AND THE SHORTCUT MENU**

- Holding down the left mouse button, highlight what you want to copy.

- Release the left button and press down the right button and release it. The shortcut menu will appear.

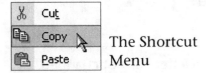 The Shortcut Menu

- Click Copy with the left mouse button.

- Click where you want the information to go in the document you are in or in a different one.

- Right-click to show the shortcut menu.

- With the left button, click Paste. (Or you can use the Paste button on the Home tab of the Ribbon.)

---

**EXERCISE 9.5 Copy Text with a Right-Click**

In this exercise, you will use the right-click and shortcut menu to copy text and paste it somewhere else.

**1.** Open the Business file with 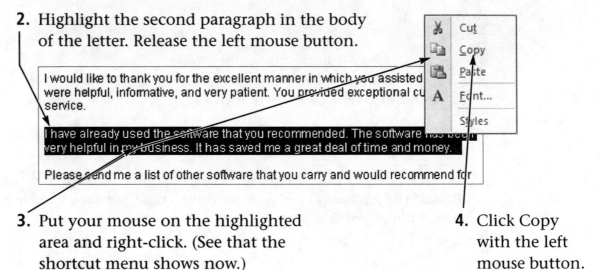→Open.

Now you will copy some text.

**2.** Highlight the second paragraph in the body of the letter. Release the left mouse button.

I would like to thank you for the excellent manner in which you assisted
were helpful, informative, and very patient. You provided exceptional cu
service.

I have already used the software that you recommended. The software has been
very helpful in my business. It has saved me a great deal of time and money.

Please send me a list of other software that you carry and would recommend for

| ✂ | Cut |
| 📋 | Copy |
| 📋 | Paste |
| A | Font... |
| | Styles |

**3.** Put your mouse on the highlighted area and right-click. (See that the shortcut menu shows now.)

**4.** Click Copy with the left mouse button.

Word copies the highlighted text The letter has not changed.

**5.** With the left button, click below the date near the top of the letter.

November 21, 2006

Ms. Juanita Thompson
Customer Service Representative
Urbana Software
810 Ivanhoe Way
Urbana, IL 61801

**6.** Right-click in the same place to bring up the shortcut menu. Click Paste with the left button.

November 21, 200

| ✂ | Cut |
| 📋 | Copy |
| 📋 | Paste |

Now you will see the sentence copied below the date, as in the following figure.

November 21, 2006
I have already used the software that you recommended. The software has been
very helpful in my business. It has saved me a great deal of time and money.

7. Highlight the sentence below the date, as shown, and press the [Delete] key to delete it.

8. Save 🖫 the Business file.

9. Choose 🔳→Close from the menu bar.
   Word closes the document but leaves the Word program open.

10. Click 🔳→New→Create to open a new blank document.
    Word creates a new blank document for the next exercise.

---

CONCEPT 9.6 **Copying from One Program to Another**

You have more choices with the documents you make if you can copy information from one program and paste it into another. You can copy pictures or text.

**HOW TO COPY FROM ONE PROGRAM AND PASTE INTO ANOTHER**

A. Open one of the programs.

B. Find and select what you want to copy.

C. Click the Copy 🖫 button or use Edit→Copy from the menu if you do not see a Copy button.

D. Open the program that you want to copy to. At this point, you will have both of the programs open. (This is called multitasking.)

E. Click where you want the information to go.

F. Click the Paste 🖫 button or use Edit→Paste from the menu if you do not see a Paste button.

**EXERCISE 9.6** **Copy from the Calculator into Word**

In this exercise, you will do a calculation on the Calculator program, copy the answer, and then paste the answer into Word.

1. Open the Calculator: Start→All Programs→Accessories→Calculator.

2. Multiply 56*10. (See steps 3–6.)

3. Click the 5 button and then the 6 button. You can see the number appear in the number box near the top of the calculator.

4. Click the multiplication sign (*).

5. Click the 1 button and then the 0 button.

6. Click the equal sign (=) to finish.

   You can see the answer (560) in the number box.

7. Click Edit→Copy from the menu bar.

   You cannot use the Copy button because the calculator does not have one.

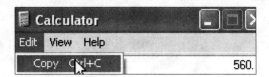

8. Click the Microsoft Word button on the Windows taskbar at the bottom of the screen. (The new blank document that you made at the end of the last exercise should be open.)

9. Type this sentence: **My answer from the calculator is**

10. Click the Paste 🖺 button. Then type a period at the end of the sentence. Your result should look like this:

    **My answer from the calculator is 560.**

11. Save 🖫 the file as **Answer**.

12. Close ⊠ the Word program.

    Use the Close button on the Word title bar.

13. Close ⊠ the Calculator program.

# Skill Builder Exercises

**Move Text by Dragging**

In this exercise, you will open a file and then you will move text in it using drag and drop.

1. Open Microsoft Word: Start→All Programs→Microsoft Office→Microsoft Office Word 2007.

2. Open the Credit file from Lesson 8. Use 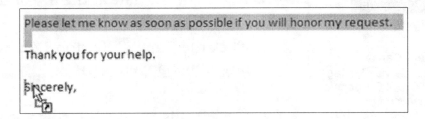→Open.

3. Highlight the third paragraph, which starts with the word "Please," and the line of space below it in the body of the letter, and then release the mouse button.

> Please let me know as soon as possible if you will honor my request.
>
> Thank you for your help.
>
> Sincerely,

4. Move your mouse onto the highlighted area, and hold down the left mouse button.

5. Keep the button down and drag until you see a small dashed line in front of "Sincerely." Now release the mouse button.

6. After you have moved that paragraph, the letter should look like this.

> Thank you for your help.
>
> Please let me know as soon as possible if you will honor my request.
>
> Sincerely,

7. Use 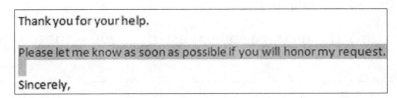→Save As to save the file as **Credit2**. Do not close the file.

**Use Undo**

In this exercise, you will practice using the Undo button to undo changes to your document.

**Before You Begin:** The Credit2 file should still be open.

1. Highlight the date at the top of the document. Click the Cut button in the Clipboard group to remove it.

2. Click the Undo 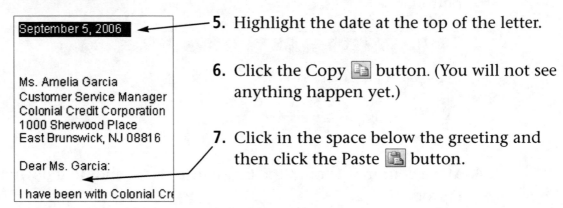 button to bring it back.

3. Highlight Amelia's first name in the inside address. Type **Gloria** to replace it.

4. Click the Undo button to change it back.

## Copy and Paste

5. Highlight the date at the top of the letter.

6. Click the Copy button. (You will not see anything happen yet.)

7. Click in the space below the greeting and then click the Paste button.

Word pastes the copied text. You might see another button below the place where you pasted. You can ignore this.

8. Click the Undo button to undo the paste.
The newly pasted text disappears.

9. Close Word. If a message appears asking if you want to save the file, click No.

---

## SKILL BUILDER 9.3  **Copy a Picture from the Internet into Word**

In this exercise, you will find a picture to copy. Then you will copy it and paste it into Word.

1. Open Internet Explorer. If you are not at Google's web page, click once in the address bar, type **google.com**, and press Enter.

2. Click the Images link.

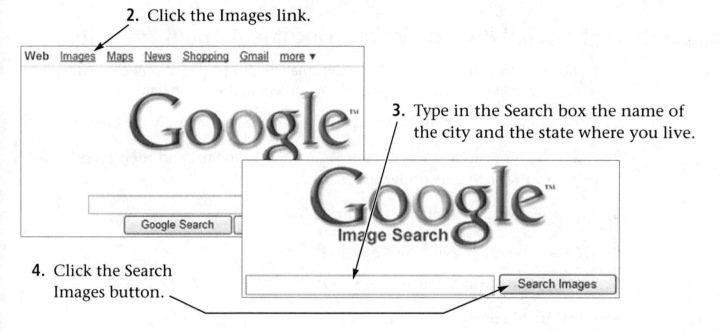

3. Type in the Search box the name of the city and the state where you live.

4. Click the Search Images button.

Google displays pictures found by your search. Now you will copy a picture.

5. Look at the pictures from the search results. Click on one picture you like.

   Google displays the small picture at the top of the page. You may also see a larger picture below the small one.

6. Right-click on the picture at the top of the page. (You will see a shortcut menu.)

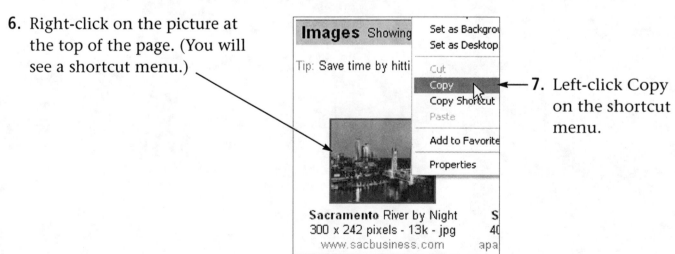

7. Left-click Copy on the shortcut menu.

8. Open Word and type the name of your city and press Enter.

9. Click the Paste button on the Home tab in the Clipboard group.

10. Save your file as **My City**.

11. Click →Print→OK to print the document, and then close the window.

---

**Personal Project: Make a Document About Your City**

In this exercise, you will create a Word document with a picture of your city and type something about the city. Then you will save and print the document.

1. Use Google to find a picture of the city or state where you were born.

2. Copy the picture into Word. Press → on the keyboard and then press Enter to get to the next line under the picture.

3. Type the name of your city and press Enter.

4. Type a paragraph that tells about that city.

5. Save the file as **Birth**.

6. Print the file using →Print .

7. Close Word. (Use the Close button on the Word title bar.)

---

 **Conversation**

## Paired Conversation

With a partner, take turns reading the A and B parts of the conversation.

| | |
|---|---|
| Student A | Greetings, my friend! |
| Student B | Hi! Are you ready for our computer lesson today? |
| Student A | Yes. I have so many files that I need to work on. |
| Student B | That's great. We can multitask today. |
| Student A | What's multitasking? |
| Student B | It means working with two or more programs at the same time. |
| Student A | Oh. That's a good word. |
| Student B | I will teach you to copy something and put it on the Clipboard. |
| Student A | And then I paste the information somewhere else, right? |
| Student B | That's right. I'll also teach you how to cut text and move it. |
| Student A | I really need to learn how to cut and move text! |
| Student B | Cut, copy, and paste are all on the Clipboard group. |
| Student A | Is the Clipboard group on the Word Ribbon? |
| Student B | Right! You seem to understand this stuff. |
| Student A | Thanks. I know the location of the files I want to work on. |
| Student B | Good. When you finish, type the new file name in the File Name box. |
| Student A | And I'll remember where I save it. |
| Student B | You're doing great. The results will be wonderful! |

# Working with Windows

## LEARNING OBJECTIVES

After studying this lesson, you will be able to:

**Computer Objectives**

- Open and use My Computer
- Use PrintScreen to print what is on the screen
- Use double-click to open computer files

**Language Objectives**

- Use vocabulary words to describe using My Computer
- Use computer verbs to describe how to use My Computer and PrintScreen
- Use computer language to talk about sorting files

*Additional learning resources are available at labpub.com/learn/esl/complit2xp/*

# Vocabulary

## Picture Dictionary

The following nouns are introduced in this lesson:

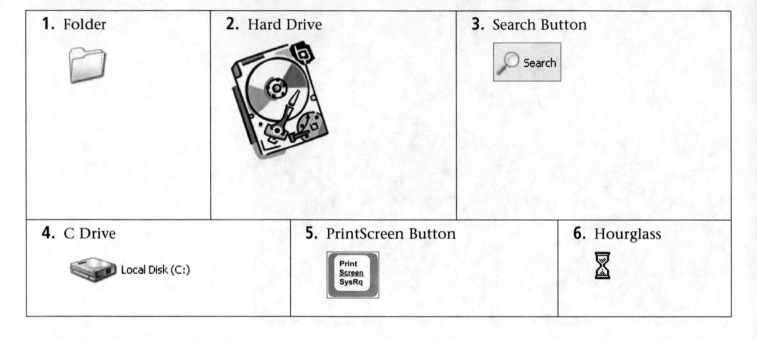

| 1. Folder | 2. Hard Drive | 3. Search Button |
|---|---|---|
| 4. C Drive | 5. PrintScreen Button | 6. Hourglass |

1. **Folder** – A place where you can organize and keep computer files

2. **Hard Drive** – This holds all the computer programs, including Windows. The information stays on the drive even when the computer is turned off

3. **Search Button** – Button that you click to start searching for a file on the computer

4. **C Drive** – A permanent hard drive inside the computer that holds the software that makes your computer work. It can hold your files

5. **PrintScreen Key** – A key on the keyboard that you can press to take a picture of the screen; puts a copy on the Clipboard

6. **Hourglass** – The symbol that may appear while the computer is working on a command

# Computer Verbs

The following verbs are introduced in this lesson:

| VERB | MEANING | EXAMPLE |
|------|---------|---------|
| 1. Double-Click | To quickly press and release the left mouse button twice | Sometimes, you need to double-click the mouse button to open a window. |
| 2. Search | A program feature that lets you look for something specific in your computer files | I forgot what I named my term paper and I need it right away. I have to conduct a search so that I can find it. |
| 3. Sort | To put things in a certain place or group according to name, size, or date | I have so many messages! I'm going to sort them by date so that I can see which ones are the newest ones. |
| 4. Modify | To make a small change to something in order to improve it | I wrote a letter yesterday, but I need to modify it because I thought of one more sentence to write in it. |
| 5. Play | Listen to a music file or watch a video file | Do you want to listen to the new music file that I downloaded from the Internet? |
| 6. Choose | To select (or to click on) something from a group of different things | My favorite colors are red, yellow, blue, and green. I have to choose one to paint my room. |
| 7. View | To look at something | I wanted to view the documents in that folder in different ways, so I clicked View on the menu. |

# Concepts and Exercises

CONCEPT 10.1 **My Computer**

In My Computer, you can see the places where files can be saved. You can also open those places to see the files that are there. (The Start menu must *not* be set to Classic View.)

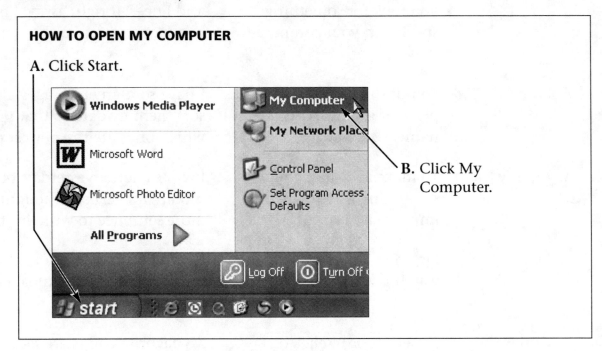

**HOW TO OPEN MY COMPUTER**

A. Click Start.

B. Click My Computer.

When My Computer opens, you will see all the places to save files on the computer.

**A. Task Pane** – Gives you choices of common places to go and actions to take on your computer.

**B. Document Folders** – File holders on the C drive where you can save and keep your files.

**C. Hard Disk** – This is a permanent disk inside the computer. The computer cannot run without it.

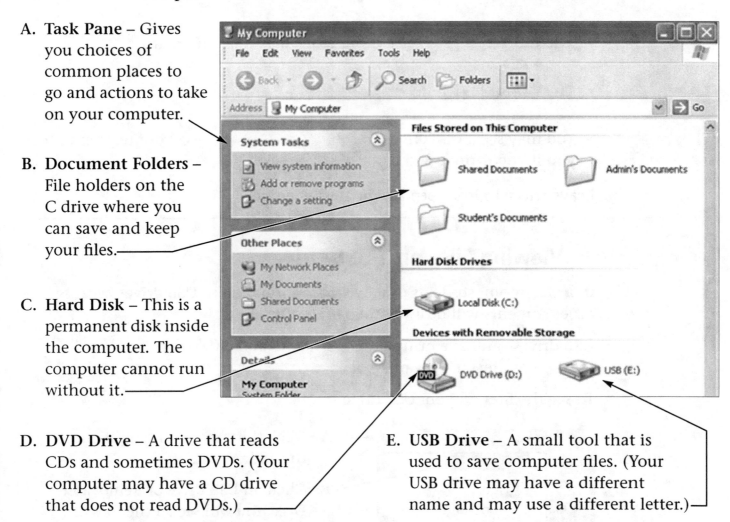

**D. DVD Drive** – A drive that reads CDs and sometimes DVDs. (Your computer may have a CD drive that does not read DVDs.)

**E. USB Drive** – A small tool that is used to save computer files. (Your USB drive may have a different name and may use a different letter.)

 EXERCISE 10.1 **Find Information in My Computer**

Windows computers have many places to save information. To see those different places, you can look in My Computer.

1. Insert your USB drive into the USB port.

2. Open My Computer: Start→My Computer or double-click it on the Desktop if you have an icon for it there.

3. Maximize ▣ the window if it does not already fill the screen.

4. Click View→Tiles. You will learn more about the View menu in Concept 10.2, Viewing Files on a USB Drive.

**5.** Look at My Computer and find:

- A folder 📁

- The C drive 💾 Local Disk (C:) (Your icons may look different.)

- The CD (or DVD) drive 💿 DVD Drive (D:)

- You may see a USB drive (E or F) 💾 Removable Disk (E:). Ask your teacher to help you if you cannot find it.

**6.** Leave this window open for the next exercise.

---

CONCEPT 10.2 **Viewing Files on a USB Drive**

In a classroom, students usually save information to USB drives because other students will be using the same computers.

USB drives can have many different names and different drive letters, but most computers usually use E or F.

To see the files on your USB drive

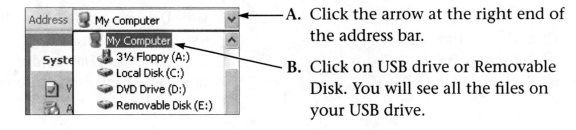

**A.** Click the arrow at the right end of the address bar.

**B.** Click on USB drive or Removable Disk. You will see all the files on your USB drive.

There are different ways that you can view files in My Computer. Here are some of the ways:

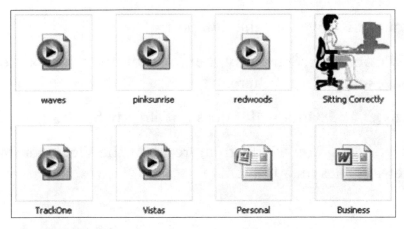

Thumbnail View

Tiles View

List View

| Name | Size | Type | Date Modified |
|---|---|---|---|
| waves | 1,890 KB | Movie file (mpeg) | 10/1/2008 9:01 |
| pinksunrise | 924 KB | Movie file (mpeg) | 10/1/2008 9:01 |
| redwoods | 2,224 KB | Movie file (mpeg) | 10/1/2008 8:59 |
| Sitting Correctly | 232 KB | Bitmap Image | 10/1/2008 8:54 |
| TrackOne | 8,509 KB | MP3 audio file (mp3) | 10/1/2008 9:05 |
| Vistas | 5,852 KB | MP3 audio file (mp3) | 10/1/2008 8:07 |
| Personal | 10 KB | Microsoft Office Word 2007 ... | 8/10/2008 7:10 |
| Business | 25 KB | Microsoft Word Document | 9/24/2006 12:0 |

Details View

The Details view shows the most information: file name, size, type of file, and more.

Notice that they are the same files, but the way that you see them is a little different.

Sometimes it is helpful to be able to sort your files in alphabetical order by name, by size, or by the date the file was last changed.

If you click on the Name heading, you sort the files in alphabetical order by name.

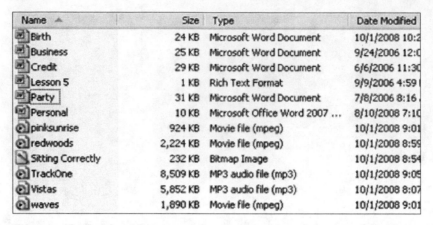

Files in Order by Name

If you click on the Size heading, you sort the files in order by size.

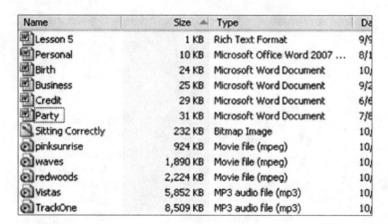

Files in Order by Size

If you click on the Date Modified heading, you sort the files in order by date and time.

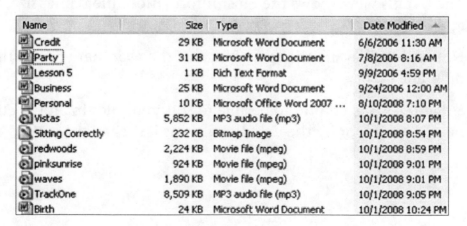

Files in Order by Date and Time

EXERCISE 10.2 **View and Sort Files**

In this exercise, you will look at the files on your USB drive. Your teacher will help you find your USB drive. Write down its name and drive letter. (For example, "Removable Drive (E:)".)

1. You should be in the My Computer window.

2. Click the arrow at the right end of the address bar.

3. Click on the USB drive to select it. You will see all the files on your USB drive. Do not worry if you do not have all the same files.

Answer    Birth    Business    Credit    Credit2    Party    Personal

4. To see information about your files, click View→Details. Look at the size, type, and date of the files. Do not worry if your sizes and dates are different.

5. Sort the files by name. Click the Name heading.

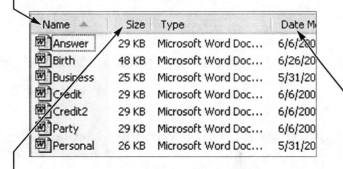

| Name ▲ | Size | Type | Date M |
|---|---|---|---|
| Answer | 29 KB | Microsoft Word Doc... | 6/6/200 |
| Birth | 48 KB | Microsoft Word Doc... | 6/26/20 |
| Business | 25 KB | Microsoft Word Doc... | 5/31/20 |
| Credit | 29 KB | Microsoft Word Doc... | 6/6/200 |
| Credit2 | 29 KB | Microsoft Word Doc... | 6/6/200 |
| Party | 29 KB | Microsoft Word Doc... | 6/6/200 |
| Personal | 26 KB | Microsoft Word Doc... | 5/31/20 |

6. Sort the files by date. Click the Date Modified heading.

7. Sort the files by size. Click the Size heading.

8. Click the ⟵ Back button to return to the My Computer window. You will see "My Computer" on the title bar.

CONCEPT 10.3 **Using Double-Click**

In My Computer and on the Windows Desktop, you must double-click the mouse to open the choices. You always use the left mouse button to double-click.

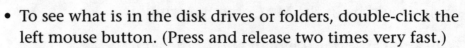

- To see what is in the disk drives or folders, double-click the left mouse button. (Press and release two times very fast.)

- When you double-click successfully, you will see the hourglass ⌛. Then a window should open and show you what is in that drive or folder.

- After you open the drive or folder, you will see the files and folders inside, if there are any.

- The type of icon each file has tells you what program it will open in.

 This icon tells you that the file will open in WordPad or one of the older versions of Microsoft Word.

 A file with this icon will open in Paint or another graphics program.

 This icon tells you that the file was made in Microsoft Word 2007.

 Files with this icon will open in Windows Media Player. They are sound, music, or video files.

 EXERCISE 10.3 **Use Double-Click to Open Files**

In this exercise, you will use double-click to open files. You should still be in the My Computer window from the last exercise.

1. Double-click the USB drive icon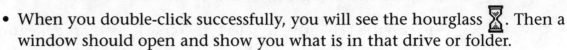

   You will see the files on your USB drive. You may have different files.

2. If you want to open one of your files, you can double-click the file icon. Look at the title bar of the program that opens. Close each program window after you look at it.

3. Click the Back button to return to My Computer.

---

## CONCEPT 10.4  Using the Task Pane

The Task Pane is on the left side of the My Computer window. It gives you choices of common places to go on the computer. You do not have to double-click to use the Task Pane. If you do not see the Task Pane, click Tools→Folder Options→Show Common Tasks in Folders→OK.

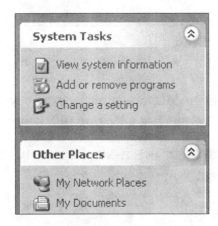

The Task Pane

 EXERCISE 10.4  **Use the Task Pane**

In this exercise, you will use the Task Pane to go to different places in the Computer.

1. Click on My Documents in the Other Places part of the Task Pane to open it. You will probably see different files.

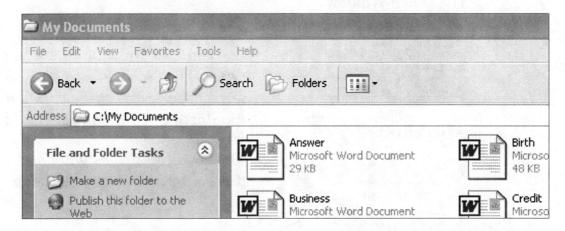

(If you want your file icons to look like this, click View→Tiles.)

2. Look at the task pane in My Documents. It has different choices than the task pane in the My Computer window.

3. Click Desktop in the task pane to see the Desktop icons.

4. Click the Back button two times to go back to My Computer.

5. Close the My Computer window.

CONCEPT 10.5 **Finding Files**

Sometimes, you may forget the name of a file you saved or where you saved it. Windows comes with a feature called Search that helps you find files.

- To open Search, click Start→Search (or open My Computer and click the Search button). Click All Files and Folders.

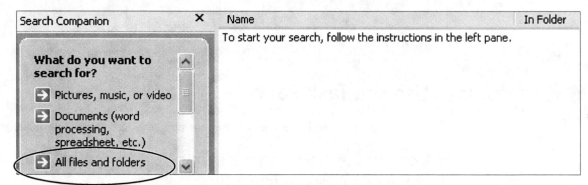

The Search Window

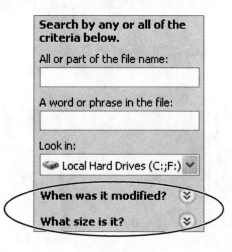

- You can look for a file by name or by the type of file. You can also go to advanced features to search by date (when it was modified) or by file size if you know it.

- The Look In box lets you choose the drive where you want to search.

EXERCISE 10.5  **Search for Files**

In this exercise, you will practice searching for files.

1. Open the Search window: Start→Search.

2. Click All Files and Folders.

3. In the top search criteria box, type **work**.

4. Click the Search button.

5. Look at the list of files that comes up. You will see all the files that have the word "work" in their name. Look at all the different kinds of icons that these files have.

6. Click View→Details.

7. Click the Size heading to put the files in order by size.

8. Click the Name heading to put the files in alphabetical order by name.

9. Close the Search window.

CONCEPT 10.6  **Using PrintScreen**

The PrintScreen key is used to print exactly what is shown on the computer screen. Some windows, like My Computer, do not have print on the menu, so the only way to print what you see is by using PrintScreen.

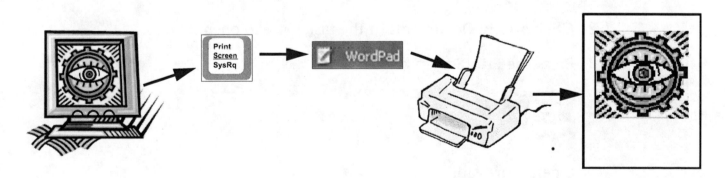

**HOW TO USE PRINTSCREEN**

A. Press the PrintScreen key on the computer keyboard. The computer just took a picture of the screen, but you won't see anything happening yet.

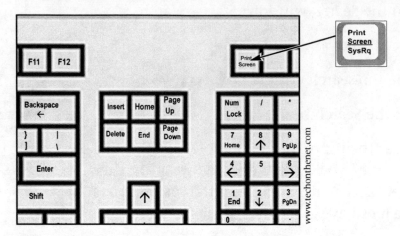

B. Open WordPad: Start→All Programs→Accessories→WordPad.

C. Click the Paste button or use Edit→Paste from the menu bar.
You will now see a picture of what was on the screen in WordPad.

D. Use File→Print to print a picture of the screen.

E. The printer prints it onto a piece of paper.

 EXERCISE 10.6 **Use PrintScreen**

In this exercise, you will print a screen from a program that does not have a print command in the menu. You can print from this program only by using PrintScreen.

1. Open My Computer: Start→My Computer.

2. Click on My Documents in the task pane to open it.

3. Press the PrintScreen key.

4. Open WordPad.

5. Click Edit→Paste.
The picture you took with PrintScreen appears on the page.

6. Click File→Print to print it onto paper.

# Skill Builder Exercises

SKILL BUILDER 10.1 **Use PrintScreen, Paste, and Print**

In this exercise, you will use PrintScreen and print a picture of your screen. (Insert your USB drive in the computer before you start this exercise.)

1. Open My Computer.

2. Double-click on the icon for your USB drive or where your teacher tells you to look for the files.

3. Click View→Details to see the files in Details view.

4. Click the Size heading to put the files in order by size with the smallest ones first.

5. Press the PrintScreen key.

6. Open WordPad. Click Edit→Paste.

7. Print the file.

8. With a pencil, circle all of the icons of Microsoft Word and WordPad files.

9. Close all windows.

**Search for Music**

In this exercise, you will search for music files and play them. (For this exercise, you will need to turn on the computer speakers before you start.)

1. Open Search by clicking Start→Search.

2. Click Pictures, Music, or Video.

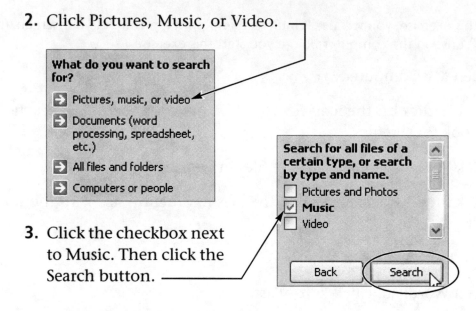

3. Click the checkbox next to Music. Then click the Search button.

4. When the results show, double-click one of the files. A sound program should open and you should hear the music.

5. When you are finished listening to the music, close the sound program using the Close button.

6. You can listen to other songs by double-clicking the files.

7. Close all windows.

**Use Search to Find a Video to Play**

In this exercise, you will search for video files and play them. (Not all computers have video files. Your teacher may put some on your classroom computers before you start. Most videos have sound so you should have the speakers turned on.)

1. Open Search: Start→Search.

2. Click on Pictures, Music, or Video.

3. Click the checkbox next to Video. Then click the Search button.

   > **Search for all files of a certain type, or search by type and name.**
   > ☐ Pictures and Photos
   > ☐ Music
   > ☑ **Video**
   >
   > [ Back ] [ Search ]

4. When the results show, double-click one of the files and you should see the video.

5. When you finish watching the video, close the video program using the Close button.

**Personal Project: Use Paint, Microsoft Word, and My Computer**

In this exercise, you will use Paint, Microsoft Word, and My Computer. (Insert your USB drive in the computer before you start this exercise.)

1. Open Paint. Create a picture of a park with trees and flowers. Save the file as **Park** on your USB drive.

2. Open Word 2007. Type the name of your new park and center it.

3. On the left, type five sentences about what you would like to have at your park. Save the file as **Park Details** on your USB drive.

4. Open My Computer.

5  Double-click on the icon for your USB drive.

6. Click View→Details to see the files in Details view.

7. Click the Date heading twice to sort them by date, with the newest ones first. Your new files should show at the top of the list.

8. Press the PrintScreen key.

9. Open WordPad. Click Edit→Paste.

10. Print the file.

# Conversation

## Paired Conversation

With a partner, take turns reading the A and B parts of the conversation.

| | |
|---|---|
| Student A | Hi. You look like you need help. |
| Student B | Yes, I do. |
| Student A | What's the problem? |
| Student B | I click the icon, but nothing happens. |
| Student A | Oh. You have to double-click it. |
| Student B | I see! I want to choose the Recycle Bin. |
| Student A | OK. You'll know it's working when you see the hourglass appear. |
| Student B | Does that mean that the program will open? |
| Student A | Yes. |
| Student B | Now I have to find my file with my important letter. |
| Student A | Is it on your C drive? |
| Student B | Yes, but I can't find it. |
| Student A | Well, we can do a search to find it. |
| Student B | Thanks. Should I click the Search button? |
| Student A | No. Click the Start button and then click Search. |
| Student B | We can play music while we wait. |
| Student A | That's a great idea. |